Executiv

For Today's

Human Resources Leader

A Practical Guide to Help You Attract & Retain Top Executive Talent

With gratitude.

Larry o.

By: Larry Comp and Steve Smith

LTC Performance Strategies, Inc.

Printed in the United States of America

Comp, Larry and Smith, Steve

Executive Compensation for Today's Human Resources Leader by Larry Comp and Steve Smith

ISBN: 9781719956857

Cover design and layout by Marleigh Miller

Warning- Disclaimer

Giving Back

In keeping with LTC Performance Strategies' values, 25% of the proceeds from sales of this book will be donated to our favorite charity: Family Promise of Santa Clarita Valley.

About Family Promise of Santa Clarita Valley

Family Promise of Santa Clarita Valley is a non-profit (501c3) public benefit organization that began operations in Santa Clarita in June of 2011 to serve homeless children and their families. Family Promise of SCV is one of over 200 affiliates across the country of Family Promise, a national nonprofit organization committed to helping low-income families achieve lasting independence. (www.familypromise.org)

Family Promise of SCV partners with over 18 local congregations of different faiths in the Santa Clarita Valley to provide overnight lodging, meals and hospitality for homeless children and their families on a 24/7, 365 basis. One of the unique aspects of Family Promise is a dedicated focus on identifying and solving the underlying causes of homelessness.

Comprehensive support services are provided to the adult family members. Each one receives intense personal and career counseling, that includes the development of a plan tailored to the specific needs of their family. This has resulted in a nearly 80% success rate in moving families back into apartments or transitional housing, so that they can return to being stable and functioning members of the community. Through Family Promise, in a few short years, dozens of local families have been able to regain and sustain their housing, independence, and dignity.

Family Promise of SCV is predominantly funded via generous donations, grants, gifts and volunteer services provided by local businesses, foundations, the faith community and citizens at large. Ongoing support of donations and volunteer service is required for Family Promise of SCV to continue to serve the families who desperately need help.

For more information or to make a donation visit: http://www.familypromiseSCV.org/

For Terry, my love and life partner.

For Colin and Conner, our greatest joy in this world.

- Larry Comp

Acknowledgements

We'd like to take a moment to thank some wonderful folks who have helped us along the way toward completing our 3rd book: Paul Falcone and Craig Duswalt for their book writing and publishing tips; **LTC Team Members**: Terry Comp, Kal Peters, Zach Hanks, Bonnie Randall, and Lisa Bailey; **Executive Benefit Partners**: Bob Nienaber, Steffen Nass, Leah Atyeo, Erin Blount, Robyn Seifert & Marla Aspinwall; **Mastermind Partners**: JoAnne Smith, Fleming Jones and Jeff Yoos; **Board Advisors**: Don Matso and Ravi Patel; **Vistage Trusted Advisors**: Marc Emmer, Dana Borowka, Sandy Barger, Janet Caldwell, Jaime Davison, Margaret Hinch, Mark Hiraide, Jeffrey Knakal, Casey Xiao-Morris, David Rice, Michael Rice and John Vance; **Vistage Chairs** who have entrusted their members to us, including: Gary Brennglass, Shel Brucker, Bob Dabic, Jed Daly, Steve Elson, Gail Shaper-Gordon, Yolanda Guibert, Rick Itzkowich, Marshall Krupp, Ron Means, Mike Miller, John Morris, Mitch Pearlman, Don Riddell, and Tom Roddell; **Professional Colleagues**: Andrew Agress, Fred Arnold, Brian Barry, Lisa Bashor, Sherry Benjamins, Jay Berger, David Bishop, Sheldon Blumling, Rob Boldt, Scott Capistrano, Bob Cohen, Barry Deutsch, Liz Egan, Robin Elledge, Gary Garbowitz, Leslie Grande, Bob Farley, Allan Fisher, Mark Fishman, Ryan Fridborg, Stephanie Granato, Christine Grimm, Mike Grover, Sheldon Harris, Calvin Hedman, Shelly Herman, Joe Herold, Sam Hicks, Mark Hoffman, Kevin Holmes, Devin Hornick, Dick Kaumeyer, Ken Keller, Diane Nott-Kilfoil, Peter Leets, Jay Lorentson, Karen Martin, Richard Martin, Barb Mather, Tony Mathews, Jeff Meyer, Aline Mirzabeigi, Brett Moisa, Scott Morsch, John Murphy, Sally Phillips, Steve Puente, Dianna Rea, Geri Rivers, Rick Rossignol, Jacque Roth, Gary Saenger, Bill Staley, DJ Stornetta, Pete Tzavalas, Kajsa Vikman, Alex Vorobieff, Eve Waldman, Scott Zimmerman; and our **700+ Valued Past & Present Clients** including: Kari Acevedo, Cliff Adams, Sonja Adams, Rebecca Barlow, Dina Barmasse, Ken Barry, Nikki Barua, Mitch Bassett, Dawn Batey, Adam Beamish, Don Bizub, Brian Blake, Chris Braun, Steve Brockmeyer, Terra Campbell, Cheryl Ceccheto, Eunice Cuadros, Michael Curtis, Pam Demond, David Demont, David Dennis, Brian Dersch, Jacky Dilfer, Barbara Doerning, Joyce Douglas, Adriana Drieman, Bassam Fawaz, Jeannie Finkel, Karyn Fish, Amber Flamminio, Julie Fleshman, Mandie Forman-Sklansky, Karla Fosburg, Jean Halsell, Ruben Galvan, Ryan Giffen, John Gray, Glenn Grindstaff, Alex Guerrero, Brett Hadley, Rob Hall, Karen Hill, Deb Horne, Auggie Huerta, Jake Johnson, Dan Jones, Jennifer Haley, Catherine Haight, Michael Hammond, Laura Hasshaw, Tylie Jones, Stuart Karten, Fred Ketcho, Sarah Kolish, Dan Kravitz, Steve Kulchin, LaTanya Justice, Chuck Landon, Alex Lopez, Freddy Lopez, Leslie Louden, Mariah Machnikowski, Reed Mack, Sandi Maimquist, Linda Mangone, Mike Mazur, Paul McMinn, Mike Morey, Karen Morris, Suzanne Moore, Elise O'Keefe, Annie Olander, Robbin Owens, Bob Passaretti, Juanita Pena, Don Perbola, Rich Phillips, Raul Porto, Mark Puleo, Steven Raft, Alex Rivera, Alison Roelke, James Roh, Tyler Savage, Candice Schmidt, Rachel Segovia, Mitchell Shack, Nick Shauer, Eric Snyder, Conor Smith, Janice Stack, Luc Stang, Mike Stark, Eric Steinhauer, Janelle Strohmeyer, Lynda Thomas, Aki Tohyama, Kimberly Toonen, Adel Villalobos, Kurt Vincelette, Sanjeev Weerasuriya, Chris Williams and Marisa Yukich.

Table of Contents

One-Hour Book Series

Most of the books you'll find on Executive Compensation are too long, too theoretical and geared to academicians and consultants. LTC Performance Strategies, Inc. created this One-Hour Book Series because today's organizational leaders have unique challenges and need answers now. They also lack the time, resources and patience to get the biggest bang for their buck in managing their organization's Total Rewards & Performance Development Programs.

This is the 3rd book in this series. The 1st 2 books are: "Thinking Inside the Box" and "Executive Compensation for Private Company CEOs and Business Owners." Each of the 1st 2 books were designed to be read within about 60 minutes. We have added additional content to this book, so it is a bit longer, but is also designed to quickly allow the reader to zero in on those chapters of greatest relevance.

We realize that having executive compensation expertise can prove to be a key competitive differentiator among today's human resource leaders. Not all of you will want to take the plunge into Executive Comp, but for those who do, we hope this simple book will provide you with a solid foundation.

About Larry Comp

Larry Comp serves as the LTC Performance Strategies' President, as well as its Practice Leader for *High Performance and Total Compensation Solutions.* Larry is a widely recognized authority in the field, having led hundreds of related initiatives in working with over 700 organizations across 50+ industry segments. These include the design, development, and implementation of:

- Executive Compensation Programs
- Executive Benefit Plans
- Salary Management Programs
- Sales Incentive Plans
- Company-wide Incentive Programs
- Long-Term Cash/ Stock-Based Plans

Larry is passionate about aligning and leveraging pay for performance relationships in order to create healthy, "high performance" companies. Client organizations frequently report increased productivity and profitability, as well as improved teamwork and ownership.

Prior to joining LTC, Larry held progressively responsible leadership roles with Baxter Healthcare, Nissan, and Babcock and Wilcox. He holds a Master's Degree in Human Resources Management, has been accredited as a Senior Professional in Human Resources (SPHR), and recognized as a Certified Management Consultant (CMC). Larry also holds the following licenses: Life and Health, Series 6, and Series 63.

In addition, Larry has co-authored over 50 articles, taught Compensation for UCLA's HR Certificate Program and served as an undergraduate and graduate adjunct professor for several universities. He has been a member of several Boards and continues to serve on the Compensation Committee of a large ESOP corporation.

About Steve Smith

Steve Smith serves as LTC Performance's Director of Client Solutions. Since joining LTC in 2009, Steve has consulted on over 300 compensation initiatives. These initiatives include the design, development, and implementation of:

- Executive Compensation Programs
  - Executive Base Pay
  - Management Incentive Plans
  - Stock and Phantom Equity Plans
  - Cash-Based Long-Term Incentive Plans
  - Executive Deferral Programs
- Sales Compensation Plans
- Company-wide Goalsharing Incentive Programs
- Salary Management Plans

Steve's passion is working closely with clients to develop solutions that allow them to utilize their Total Compensation Program to attract and retain top caliber talent, while realizing a solid return on investment. Steve strives to ensure clients' plans achieve a strong pay for performance relationship, while being externally competitive and internally equitable.

Steve holds a Master's Degree in Business Administration (MBA) from Woodbury University and a Bachelor's Degree in Business Administration/ Business Law from California State University, Northridge.

Introduction

Today's HR leaders face unique challenges every day, such as:

"I need to hire a CFO. What will we have to pay this person?"

"Everyone's talking about the importance of building a pay for performance culture...how do we get there?"

"My Head of Sales and Marketing just asked for equity...do we really need to offer her a piece of the pie?"

We're thinking about selling our company...what can we do to retain our key leaders through this process?"

These are the types of questions that are frequently asked. Today's Human Resource leaders need answers, and typically right away! Quite often, they are not sure where to turn.

The field of Executive Compensation is dynamic and highly complex, and sometimes having a little information is dangerous! As accounting rules, labor legislation, the global economy and competitive practices evolve, it's beneficial for today's HR Leaders to have an independent advisor(s) who is readily accessible and one they can trust. Unfortunately, many such advisors lack the necessary depth and breadth of experience to provide customized solutions for organizations like yours. Others may be unduly expensive.

You may have a specific executive compensation problem and, if so, can immediately refer to the related chapter. However, because of the interrelatedness of the various topics covered, you may benefit from a quick read of the entire book. (The book can be read in about 90 minutes, providing you with key tools, tips, insights, and guidelines you need to manage your most important investment.)

If you're starting to develop your executive compensation program from scratch, the following model will provide you with a "big picture" overview of how you might get from where you are, to where you want to be.

Analysis of Executive Compensation Trends

↓

Formulation of Compensation Positioning Philosophy

↓

Determination of Program Objectives

↓

Clarification of Executive Roles

↓

Analysis of Competitive Pay Levels & Practices

↓

Assessment of Internal Equity Considerations

↓

Determination of "Mix" of Total Compensation Components

↓

Establishment of Base Salary Levels

↓

Development of Short-Term Incentive Plan

↓

Development of Long-Term Incentive Plan

↓

Review of Executive Benefit Alternatives; Evaluation of Appropriate Capital Accumulation Vehicle

↓

Design Of Program Communications

Chapter 1

Managing Your Biggest Investment

We are grateful to have had the opportunity to consult with over 700 organizations across industry. In asking our clients about their biggest expense, we almost always get the same response: "COMPENSATION."

Until a few years ago, most companies paid less attention to managing executive compensation. However, the 2008 recession seemed to wake us all up. Today, most organizations are pretty serious about getting the "biggest bang from their buck" on their executive compensation programs.

Given the highly-competitive job market we have been experiencing, most organizational leaders fear an increase in voluntary employee turnover. Since the cost of turnover isn't readily apparent on the Profit and Loss Statement, it hasn't, historically, received the attention it deserves. However, when you consider the cost of replacing an executive: search fees, time spent in the recruitment/ screening process, loss of knowledge, disruption to the business...it all adds up. In fact, the cost of voluntary executive turnover can well exceed 100% of the replaced executive's salary.

Over the last several years, many Chief Executives and Human Resource Officers have shifted their perspective. Instead of viewing compensation as an expense, they now consider it an investment. Please note that while it's hard to pinpoint specific findings that quantify compensation's return on investment (ROI), a study was conducted that produced a model contrasting the productivity of top vs. average performers. Below is an excerpt pertaining to management/ professional workers:

- "Average" workers' productivity = 48% more than "Non-producers"
- "Superior" workers' productivity = 48% more than "Average"
- "Superior" workers' productivity = 96% more than "Non-producers" (Beek)

Michael Sturman conducted a second study of this nature. In his study, he evaluated the economic value added to an organization from above average, average and below average performers. Below are the conclusions from this study:

- "Average" performers' economic value added = 11x more than "Below Average"
- "Above Average" performers' economic value added = 2x more than "Average"
- "Above Average" performers' economic value added = 21x more than "Below Average" (Sturman, 2003)

So what these studies imply is that if you're not hiring top-notch performers, you are costing yourself a lot of money.

In our current era, companies have to get more done with fewer employees. This has made competition for the best and the brightest, tougher and tougher. Since compensation is a primary reason why executives choose to join or leave an organization, doesn't it make sense to ensure that your compensation program helps you to attract, engage, motivate and retain those executives who can take your company to increasingly higher levels

Chapter 2

Paying for Performance

About 15 years ago, I (Larry) was intrigued by an article that came across my desk. It described a comprehensive study in which the prominent firm, Bain Consulting, asked CEOs across the country, to: (1) think about all of the various initiatives they had undertaken to drive their companies forward, and (2) to select the one that had provided them with the greatest return on investment (ROI). As I began to skim the article I couldn't help chuckling to myself, because so many of us CEOs and business owners operate by MMA (Management by Magazine Article). That being the case, I quickly scanned the rest of the article to discover the results of this study. Of course, the list included the typical initiatives we all tend to think about- management by objectives, customer segmentation, continuous improvement, and the like. But, guess what the #1 most cited initiative was? "PAY FOR PERFORMANCE."

OK, as an executive compensation consultant, I have to admit that I was very pleased to learn of this research finding. But I had to be honest and ask myself, would pay for performance stand the test of time…or was this just another passing fad? Well, the study was repeated later with PFP again coming in #1.

Now, 15+ years later, we're finding that this topic just continues to get hotter and hotter.

You see, in the past, pay levels were largely linked to employee tenure, and annual pay raises were pegged to a cost-of-living index. Of course, these COL increases had no linkage to performance and, therefore, provided a weak return on investment.

In years gone by, it was also unusual for anyone but executives to qualify for annual bonuses. And when bonuses were provided, these were typically discretionary. Of course, discretionary bonuses lack the potency needed to incent the desired performance and behavior.

Well, this has all changed over the last several years. Leading companies are now tying virtually all forms of compensation to performance. Merit increases are now predominantly linked to individual performance. Short-Term Incentive Plans now cover most employees across the organization and are strongly linked to organizational and individual performance. Long-Term Incentive Plans (i.e. stock options or cash-based LTIPs) are typically offered to the key strategic leaders and are primarily linked to longer-term performance measures. Today, even many of our executive benefit plans incorporate a pay for performance feature.

As companies implement effective pay for performance programs, they improve organizational alignment, employee engagement and motivation, financial performance and the value and attractiveness of the enterprise.

Building a pay for performance culture can be very rewarding, but also quite challenging. We all remember the Law of Physics, right? "For every action there is an equal and opposite reaction." Many people might say that they look forward to change, yet in reality, most people resist it. Therefore, when you set out to create a healthy, higher performing company, you'll need a strong plan and a firm commitment to holding yourself and your executive team accountable for making this goal a reality. Let's look at some tips you will want to consider.

1. **Commit to creating a positive, progressive culture.**

People want to work in an environment where they are trusted and respected. If you give them the right tools and proper guidance, they will often pleasantly surprise you.

2. **Develop a "growth" mindset.**

In this age of global competition and accelerated change, good is no longer good enough. We need to get out of our incremental thinking and take our businesses to higher levels.

3. **Focus on profitable growth.**

Whether we realize it or not, all chief executives bring their own biases toward driving profitability. Some focus on sales and tend to see growth opportunities everywhere. Others focus on cost containment/ expense reduction. Which is the proper orientation? You're right... BOTH.

4. **Get everyone on the same page.**

Most of us have probably been involved in strategic planning. You remember---you go off site for a day or so and come back with a zillion ideas and a notebook full of charts and graphs. And yes, the notebook ends up sitting on a shelf with the information never being shared with the troops. Look to reduce your plan to a page and share whatever you can with your employees, so they can be part of "the game of business."

5. Work smart: focus on the vital few.

Many companies have no clear-cut goals. Some have dozens and change these frequently, which ends up driving everyone nuts. Pick the 5-7 most important financial and non-financial goals. Make sure everyone is aligned with these goals and going in the right (read, *same*) direction.

6. Build a company of business people

Make sure you have the right people in the right roles. Help them to understand business, especially your own business. For your executives and other employees to be able to select the proper goals, they need to understand the big picture and what you see as important. They also need to see how the work they do makes a difference in the overall performance of the organization.

7. Give them a stake in the outcome

Without building an entitlement culture, give your people an opportunity to earn good bonuses for strong organizational and individual performance. Help them understand what they need to do to help the company, as well as themselves, be successful.

8. Hold each other accountable/ execute

People are all too familiar with the "program of the month." Don't be surprised if they are not too excited with your new initiative to create a pay for performance culture. They've been through other initiatives before and know that, oftentimes, things just go back to "normal," no matter how dismal that sounds. To achieve the desired results, you need to make sure that all of your managers are on board and are being held accountable. Remember, the biggest reason top executives fail is that they fail to execute. Don't become another statistic.

The concept of pay for performance is, simply put, difficult to disagree with. This is the main reason it is being integrated into all facets of total compensation. Given the fact that compensation is generally an organization's largest investment, doesn't it make sense to design your total compensation plan in a way that gives you the biggest bang for your buck?

Chapter 3

Establishing Your Executive Compensation Philosophy

During the early 1990s, I (Larry) served as an HR leader with a highly respected, global medical device company. We were on a hiring spree, and like our competitors, intent on attracting the best candidates. Of course, these candidates, in turn, were looking to work for the best companies. Occasionally, one of them would ask me about our Company's compensation philosophy and I would proudly state that we paid at the 75th percentile, which means that we were paying more than 75% of the other companies within our respective market.

One day it occurred to me that our employment value proposition, cited above, might not be all that unique. In fact, all of our competitors seemed to be using the same spiel. You know, "we pay at the 75th percentile." Whoa, was that even mathematically possible?

Anyway, one day it seemed like Corporate America woke up to the realization that paying salaries at the 75th percentile wasn't such a great idea. In essence, all we were doing was driving up our fixed costs. What we needed to do was contain these fixed expenses so we could allocate more of our total compensation budget to incentive pay, which is a variable expense.

So what did we all do in an effort to differentiate ourselves from the competition? Yep, you guessed it: we all changed our positioning philosophies to, once again, follow one another. Now we all seem to be pegging our pay levels to the 50th percentile.

Of course, when we say 50th percentile, it's not quite that simple. Companies must consider each of the total compensation components (salary, short-term incentive, long-term incentive, benefits) that comprise their total compensation packages and decide how they intend to allocate dollar values across each of these components.

As you read further, you'll gather tips and ideas on how to structure each portion of your total compensation package. But the important thing to note right now is that each portion of the mix represents a significant investment and should be tailored to meet your organization's specific requirements.

Now if you were to try to articulate how many of today's forward-thinking companies are positioning their compensation levels, it might look something like this: base salaries at or slightly below the 50th percentile, salaries plus target incentives, at or somewhat above the 50th percentile. These companies then, typically, *leverage* their pay for performance plans in order to contain their fixed expenses (salaries), while offering significant variable pay incentives for superior results. This type of positioning sends a strong message that these companies are serious about their businesses and willing to pay generously for the desired results.

For the record, let's clarify that the 50th percentile is not necessarily a figure that is cast in stone. It depends on many variables such as the size and type of companies you are benchmarking your company against, as well as the particular survey sources you are utilizing. We'd also like to suggest that you guard against oversimplification here. In other words, before you lock yourself into a particular compensation positioning philosophy, ask yourself some key questions such as:

- What is our company's stage of evolution? For instance, are we a "start-up" or a mature organization?
- Are we offering a long-term compensation component, or just salary and an annual incentive?
- What are we able to afford at this time?

Once you have determined your compensation positioning philosophy, we then suggest formulating a set of associated program objectives. These objectives will serve as a foundation for your executive compensation program. Your set might include objectives such as:

- Attract and retain top caliber executives
- Incent the desired organizational and individual performance
- Be externally competitive and internally equitable
- Ensure a strong pay for performance relationship
- Comply with applicable regulations

You can then step back, each year, to assess your executive compensation program against your stated objectives. This will allow you to see where you've been successful, as well as where any improvements may be needed in the future.

In an effort to be more helpful here, we have taken the opportunity to provide you with a sample Compensation Philosophy and Objectives Statement, which you will find in the Appendix.

In the meantime, the teeter-totter diagram below will serve as a gentle reminder that managing compensation, your company's largest investment, is no easy matter. Compensation is both an art and a science, and managing it requires a delicate balance. In essence, you need to pay enough to attract, motivate and retain top talent, while at the same time, manage associated costs to achieve a strong return on total compensation dollars expended.

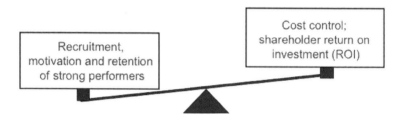

Chapter 4

Clarifying Your Roles

Despite all the testimonies we hear about the productivity of the U.S. workforce, our organizations are nowhere near as productive as they could be. Conservative estimates indicate that the average employee wastes as much as 25% or more of his/ her time each day (Wow!). While some of this is due to not doing things right the first time, much of the problem stems from working on low priority items…or on work that no longer needs to be done.

The above paragraph may have conjured up a picture in your mind of a bunch of ineffective, lower level, nonexempt employees. Sure, some of these individuals are not as productive as they could be, but chances are they have a pretty good idea of what they're supposed to do…and they also tend to be pretty closely supervised. But what about some of the executives you may have hired along the way. Aren't they supposed to know what to do…and what to focus on? Well sure, but they tend to have a lot more discretion in carrying out their roles. Chances are, they may be out of sync with the CEO and with one another.

A factor that often compounds this problem in smaller organizations is that many of their executives fulfill multiple roles. For example, consider a financial executive who heads up IT, or a Human Resources executive who also manages facilities and payroll. These "hybrid" roles are not nearly as common in the larger publicly traded companies that have the size and resources to allow their executives to be more specialized. So, while it is often more efficient for smaller private companies to utilize hybrid roles, care must be taken to ensure that such roles and their associated responsibilities are well defined.

Try this exercise: Ask one of your executives to independently make a list of what he/ she considers to be his/ her key job responsibilities in order of priority. Then ask your CEO to put together the same list, in terms of how he/she sees the executive's priorities. Once they've both completed their lists, exchange them and compare answers. Chances are, you may find that the two of them aren't on the same page. Of course it's better to learn this sooner than later. If you've found that your executive, who is earning $100,000 per year is wasting or misdirecting 20% of his/ her time, you may have just saved your company $20,000. However, this figure is actually understated, because it doesn't recognize the compounding effect of this problem; nor does it recognize the opportunity costs missed by focusing on some of the wrong priorities. According to a *USA Today* Report, CEO tenure has declined from 10 years to about 5.5 years since the 1990's (Petrecca & Strauss, 2012). Another study shows a drop of an additional year since 2013 (Harvard, 2018). Many of these executives have been "let go." We wonder how much of this turnover may be due to misunderstandings about roles, goals and priorities?

Ok, so we've just focused on the importance of clarifying the executive role. However, each executive's success is largely due to the collective efforts and contributions of his/ her employees. Therefore, doesn't it make sense for each executive to make sure his/ her employees' roles are also clear and well-aligned?

Thankfully, many conflicts can be avoided by clarifying roles at the time of hire. Here are some simple tools to consider in remedying related problems:

Job Descriptions

Job descriptions are generally multiple page documents that summarize the purpose of each role and clarify key responsibilities and position requirements. For many positions, responsibilities can be listed in order of priority or time expended. For jobs that follow a specific routine, responsibilities can be listed in chronological order.

Mini Profiles

Mini Profiles are much more concise than traditional job descriptions. Both describe organizational roles and requirements, but the mini profiles do so in a much more abbreviated manner.

In the past, most of our clients opted for job descriptions. They realized that the additional detail that job descriptions provide could help them to be more effective when it came to executing key business activities such as recruitment, selection, orientation, coaching and performance development. On the other hand, job descriptions take more time to prepare and are difficult to keep current for organizations experiencing a great deal of change, and/ or operating with a lean Human Resources staff. For such organizations, mini profiles may prove to be the most viable tool.

Based upon your company's specific requirements, you may choose to utilize job descriptions, mini profiles, or both.

Whichever approach you decide to use to clarify your employees' roles, here are a few benefits you should realize:

- Staff members will feel more secure
- The organization will realize greater synergy
- The likelihood of related conflicts will decrease
- Productivity (and profits) will increase
- You will enjoy more positive relations with your staff

As organizational leaders, we often resist structure. Some of us may even see job descriptions as limiting. But here's where we may benefit from looking at the world from the perspective of our staff members. The majority of these individuals want to do a good job for us. Most come to work for more than a paycheck: many relish the opportunity to contribute to something bigger than themselves---to make a difference. This can better be accomplished when staff members have a clear understanding of what is expected of them. As leaders, we may be pleasantly surprised to see employee motivation take off when staff members begin feeling more confident and competent that they are performing well, and indeed making their contribution.

We have taken the opportunity to provide you with job description and job profile templates, which you will find in the Appendix.

Chapter 5

Paying the Right Salaries

Establishing appropriate executive salaries is often challenging. Pay too low of a salary and you'll find it quite difficult to attract and retain the type of talent necessary to drive your organization forward. However, pay too much and you'll simply be increasing your fixed expenses and cutting into your bottom line, without any correlation to performance.

A typical request we receive from a client looking for assistance in coming up with an appropriate candidate salary, might sound something like this:

Client: Hi Steve, my name is Fred Munoz. I'm the CEO of a company called Scott Electronics. My friend, Bill Leon, said you were able to help him navigate through some difficult Compensation challenges. I was wondering if you might be able to do the same for me?

Steve: Bill's a great guy; appreciate his referral. How can I help, Fred?

Client: Well, my Controller, Sally Hernandez just resigned. She's been with us for 10 years. I need to replace her ASAP, but have no idea what to pay for this position. Sally always seemed content with her salary, but informed me that she is leaving for a better offer.

Steve: I see. Can you tell me a bit about your company, Fred, so I can better understand your situation?

Client: Sure. We're a 15-year old private company. We manufacture electronic components for the defense industry. We've been growing about 10% per year and see some "untapped" opportunity to capture greater market share.

Steve: Thanks, Fred. How many employees do you have and what is your projected revenue?

Client: We have about 100 employees; approximately 80 at headquarters, with the rest of our folks working out of various field *locations. We did about $18M in revenue and expect to break $20M this fiscal year.*

Steve: *Great, thanks. Where is your company headquartered?*

Client: *We're located just outside of Miami.*

Steve: *Thanks, Fred. In Sally's role as your Controller, was she your top financial executive?*

Client: *Yes.*

Steve: *Had you ever considered her for a CFO role?*

Client: *Well, no… I sort of play that role. She was more of a tactical player. You know, very good at managing the basic accounting functions and getting our reports completed on time.*

Steve: *Did Sally have any responsibilities outside of your Accounting Department?*

Client: *Oh yes, she oversaw HR and our IT functions, as well as our receptionist and some of our administrative employees.*

Steve: *Sounds like your managers may need to wear a lot of hats.*

Client: *That's right…we're all spread pretty thin.*

Steve: *Would you consider bringing in a CFO if you found the right person, or would you prefer to keep that responsibility and bring in another Controller?*

Client: *Interesting question, Steve- yes I might. That could free me up to work on some higher- level strategic priorities.*

Steve: *Can you tell me a little bit about any short-term incentive plans you offer?*

Client: *Well, quite frankly, our plan needs some work. Right now, we tie any incentive payouts to performance against our annual profitability target. I also have the discretion to adjust any bonuses at the end of the year. Sally's bonus incentive target has been 15% of her salary. We've paid close to target the last few years.*

Steve: Do you provide any equity or other types of long-term compensation?

Client: No, but, confidentially, we are thinking about selling the company within the next 5-7 years. I may need to offer some type of long-term incentive plan for retention purposes, as well as rewarding some of our key strategic leaders for driving longer-term performance and increasing the value and attractiveness of our company.

Steve: Thanks Fred, this has been very helpful. Anything else I need to know at this point?

Client: No, I think this pretty much covers it. What do you propose?

Steve: Well, based on your parameters, we could research Controller positions for comparable companies within the Miami geographical market. We will also factor in the additional responsibilities that your controller has. If you like, we could also include survey data for a CFO position. We would provide you with benchmark reports from reputable sources; this would include salaries at the 25th, 50th and 75th percentiles, along with the incentive & total cash compensation data at the same percentiles. If you like, we could also include some information on long-term compensation practices, since you are concerned about long-term retention.

Client: Sounds great, Steve. What are the next steps?

Steve: Of course, Fred. How about if we carve out some time in the next few days to debrief on our findings and discuss some alternative approaches to putting together a compensation package?

Client: Excellent, Steve, talk to you then.

Coming up with appropriate executive salaries, in some respects, is easier for publicly traded companies. First of all, there is a lot more competitive survey information available for these organizations. Second, public companies are now required to detail the total compensation packages of their 5 highest paid executives in their annual Proxy Statements. This information is available to the public.

Smaller and medium-sized private companies are, therefore, at a disadvantage when it comes to identifying comparable pay data and developing appropriate executive compensation recommendations. However, competitive market data is available for anyone willing to purchase the information. A note of caution, however; the cost and quality of these surveys varies considerably.

Once the company has established its executive compensation positioning philosophy (chapter 3), it is then time to put the numbers behind it. For executives, total compensation generally consists of three variables: 1) salary, 2) short-term incentives/ bonuses and 3) long-term incentives.

Let's assume for a moment that a company decides its compensation philosophy is to target total compensation (salary + short-term incentives + long-term incentives) at the 50th percentile. Well, that's fine in concept, but now real data needs to be gathered for each role in order to ascertain what these percentiles mean in terms of actual dollars.

There are 4 major variables to be aware of that influence executive compensation levels. The first and foremost is the role. This, of course, can be fairly straightforward or, in the case of hybrid or unique roles, can be somewhat complex. This is why proper role clarification is crucial prior to developing external market compensation data. The other major variables are, in order of general influence: company size, location, and industry. These parameters must first be identified before moving forward with the gathering of compensation data, which is often called "benchmarking."

1. Role: For obvious reasons, the role is the most critical factor influencing executive compensation. Each position carries its own unique responsibilities & required qualifications. The external market, as well as the internal hierarchy, will dictate that certain roles be compensated greater than others.

2. Company Size: Generally speaking, the larger the company the greater executives are compensated. Although there are several reasons why this is the case, it generally comes down to scope. For example, the head of human resources in a company employing thousands of people will have a "bigger" job than one in a 100-employee company. Generally, revenue & employee count are the most common expressions of company size and a comparable range to look at might be companies within ½ to 2 times that of the company in question.

3. Location: In real estate it is all about three things: location, location, location. However, in executive compensation there is somewhat of a misnomer that location doesn't matter since the talent pool is nationwide or even global. The reality is that if a company has an executive in Mississippi & wants to relocate them to New York City, you better bet that executive will want a raise. So this is fairly evident proof that location should be considered. Certain labor markets demand more pay than others, so this is another factor to consider when evaluating compensation data.

4. Industry: Let's face it, some industries pay better than others! Sometimes there is good reason for it, sometimes not. Often times it simply comes down to profit margins and affordability. Certain industries are known for low salaries & large incentive opportunities, and vice versa for other industries. When determining how to pay an executive, companies always want to find out what their direct competitors pay their executives. This is a very valid concern. However, it is often times important to also look at a broader perspective, rather than only looking at a very narrow subset of industry. When companies focus in too narrowly, they can sometimes get in the "rut" of simply copying the competitors, rather than differentiating themselves. If there is a better practice out there, why not explore it...why not be a leader, rather than a follower?

In regard to industry, it is also important to consider whether industry really matters to the role you are assessing. Perhaps for the COO, knowledge of the industry is key and therefore the talent pool is limited to those with industry background. But what about the Chief IT Officer? In certain circumstances that individual does not need industry expertise, so why limit that data pool to only IT executives in your industry?

Once survey benchmarking data has been gathered, the decision then has to be made regarding what to pay each executive based on the company's compensation positioning philosophy, the experience/ skill set of the individual in question and various other internal & external factors. Salaries are often the first component that a company and job candidate will focus in on, so offering an appropriate salary will be a key foundational element in a well-rounded total compensation package. Additionally, salaries are generally the only form of compensation that is "guaranteed," accordingly, salaries need to be high enough to provide the executive with an appropriate "standard of living," while leaving enough "on the table" in order to incorporate attractive pay-for-performance incentive components.

The graphs below, from Economic Research Institute (Economic Research Institute, 2018), illustrate the effect each of the above-mentioned variables has on a CEO's salary.

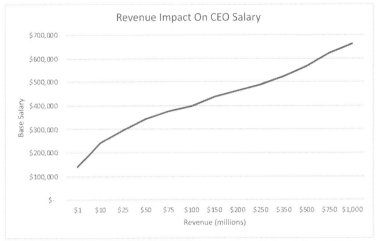

Source: Economic Research Institute, All Industry Data; National (Aug. 2018)

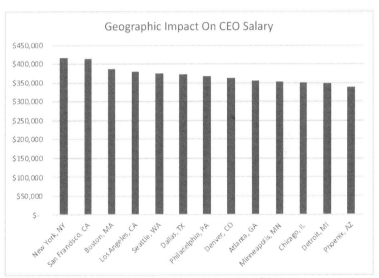

Source: Economic Research Institute, All Industry Data; $50M Revenue
(Aug. 2018)

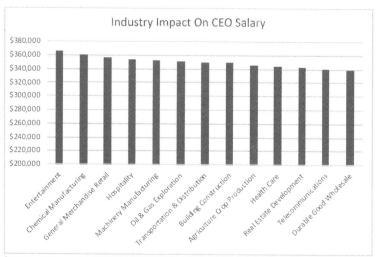

Source: Economic Research Institute, National Data; $50M Revenue (Aug. 2018)

As the head of human resources in your organization, you may wish to consider purchasing a few appropriate surveys to help you assess the market competitiveness of your executive pay packages. While there are several free sources of benchmarking data available these days (i.e. Salary.com, Glassdoor, etc.), many of these free sources have significant limitations when it comes to benchmarking roles, particularly executive roles. As such, more and more organizations are choosing to outsource this function, rather than purchasing the reports themselves or relying upon limited and/or questionable data available via free resources.

One reason is time. It often takes a good bit of time to get up to speed in learning how to effectively utilize many of these surveys & to understand how to match up your company roles with the survey roles. A second reason is cost. Many of these surveys are fairly expensive and require annual subscriptions. A third reason is the analysis itself. No single survey source is perfect. Sample sizes, the makeup of companies within the sample, and survey methodologies all vary from one source to the next. The fourth reason is reliability. Quality survey data needs to be gathered from top notch survey sources in order to be trusted and relied upon.

A qualified executive compensation specialist can help you determine which surveys are best for evaluating your various positions, and how to make sense of the various compensable factors: (i.e. location, size, industry, company's stage of evolution, positioning philosophy, role, scope, incumbent/ candidate experience and training, internal equity).

Chapter 6

Handling Pay Increases

A few years ago, I (Steve) designed a salary administration program for a prominent, global distribution client. In reviewing their salary data, I was shocked to learn that some of their hourly-paid stock clerks were earning around $70,000 per year, and in a very low paying area of the U.S. In essence, they were being paid about 3X as much as many of the other employees in their same job classification.

When we inquired about why these individuals were paid so well, we found out that these 30+ year employees had received the "normal" pay increases every year they were employed. This practice, of course, resulted in their being significantly overpaid for their particular role. (Can you imagine the financial impact of this same practice being applied to a group of long-term executives?)

In years gone by, average annual executive merit increases were in neighborhood of 8%. However, when companies began focusing on holding down fixed costs (salaries) and allocating more of the total pay "mix" to variable pay, increase percentages began to dwindle. The projected salary increase average for 2018 is approximately 3% ((SHRM), 2018). This average has held constant over the past several years.

Since the last economic recession, the job market has significantly rebounded. We are now hearing more and more stories about individual job candidates who are receiving multiple job offers. With this turnaround in the job market, astute CEOs and business owners are now quite concerned about losing their higher performing executives and, therefore, are finding creative ways to retain them. For instance, while most U.S. companies are budgeting in the neighborhood of 3% for their merit increase pools, some are quietly singling out their "star" performers and granting them significantly larger pay increases.

Given the increasing importance of pay for performance, many companies have developed simple administrative tools, such as Merit Increase Allocation Matrices to more intelligently and effectively allocate their limited annual merit increase dollars. Such tools are built around an annual merit budget. Any merit increases are then granted based upon: (1) where employees are paid within their pay range (compa-ratio) and (2) their individual performance rating.

We developed the sample matrix below to illustrate how budgeted increase dollars could be allocated in a more efficient, objective, consistent and cost-effective manner. To calculate an employee's compa-ratio, find his/her annualized salary and the midpoint of the Company's corresponding pay grade (or the survey data focal point in the absence of a pay grading system). Then simply divide the employee's pay rate by the mid-point to get his/her compa-ratio (see illustration below). To then find the employee's recommended pay increase, locate the appropriate compa-ratio on the vertical axis and move horizontally across the row to the column corresponding to the employee's appraisal rating.

Compa-Ratio		INCREASE PERCENTAGE			
MAX 115 - 120		0.0	1.0	2.0	3.0
106 - 114		0.0	2.0	3.0	4.0
MID 95 - 105	No Increase until performance improves	0.0	3.0	4.0	5.0
86 - 94		0.5	3.5	4.5	5.5
80 - 85 MIN		1.0	4.0	5.0	6.0
	Unsatisfactory	Opportunity For Improvement	Effective	Highly Effective	Distinguished

To calculate an employee's Compa-ratio, find his/her base pay and the midpoint of the corresponding pay grade on the Company's Pay Structure. Then divide the pay rate by the midpoint (see illustration below). To then find the employee's recommended pay increase, locate the appropriate comp-ratio and move across the row to the column corresponding with the employee's appraisal rating.

Example:

Salary	$	150,000	0.91	Appraisal Rating = Effective
Midpoint	$	165,000		Merit Increase = 3.50%

The sample Merit Increase Allocation Matrix (above) incorporates 5 performance rating levels. Each company utilizes different performance rating descriptors. Some may utilize 5, like the sample above. Others may utilize 3,4, 6, or even more. Regardless, the intent is the same: utilize the tool to: (1) link pay to performance, while keeping rising salaries in check, and (2) accelerate the movement of lower paid, higher performing employees.

Company executives, managers, supervisors, and other employees tend to like this type of Merit Increase tool since it enhances the objectivity and consistency of the salary administration process.

Chapter 7

Driving the Appropriate Performance and Behavior (Short-Term Incentives)

"Building a visionary company requires 1% inspiration and 99% alignment." – Jim Collins and Jerry Porras, "Built to Last"

Some years ago, Bain Consulting (Bain Consulting) conducted a survey of CEOs across the country to discover which ones of the initiatives they had been focusing on (i.e. strategic planning, total quality management, customer segmentation, outsourcing) had delivered the best financial results. Of the 25 initiatives listed below, pay for performance came out #1! Since that time, pay for performance has continued to grow in importance, especially with respect to short-term (performance of ≤1 year) incentive plans.

With competition becoming more and more intense, progressive leaders have found that short-term incentive plans, when properly designed and administered, are an organization's most potent vehicle for driving the desired performance and behavior. Below are some of the benefits reported from well-designed plans:

- Increased revenue
- More efficient processes
- Decreased costs
- Increased skills/ knowledge
- Enhanced quality
- Improved motivation/ teamwork
- Improved customer satisfaction

The above benefits are quite compelling and probably the reason why so many companies (including almost all of our clients) offer short-term incentive opportunities to all of their employees.

For optimal results, leading companies typically kick off their short-term incentive programs by focusing and aligning the executive team with a handful of critically important (annual) financial and non-financial goals. The success of the organization can then be largely attributed to how well the executives, as well as the employees working for these leaders, execute their responsibilities. That's why it is so important to have the right executive talent properly focused, aligned and accountable from the start.

Each organization must decide which performance measure(s) to include in their respective short-term incentive plans. While some companies may just select one measure, others may choose a dozen or so. Most of the companies we have worked with on the design of their STI plans have selected 5-7 goals. We find that 5-7 goals allow the company to focus employees on a broad range of objectives, without overwhelming them and/or watering down the focus on any particular goal. We believe that these goals, where appropriate, should include financial, as well as non-financial goals and that these should be weighted appropriately. Of course, each company's goals may change from year to year depending on their specific circumstances. The chart below, from a 2016 study, illustrates performance measurements utilized by private company participants (WorldatWork, 2016):

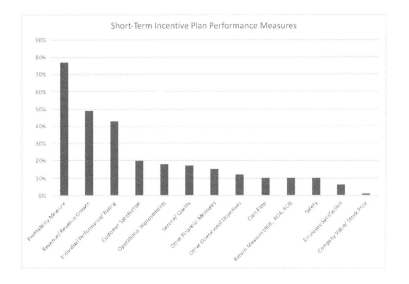

For several decades, we've worked closely with our clients on the design and implementation of their short-term incentive programs, and they've always experienced positive results. About 15 years ago, we read about a "breakthrough" goal-setting and incentive methodology called Goalsharing, which had delivered some *incredible* results. Apparently, a consultant first introduced the concept of Goalsharing to Corning. Listed below are some of the extraordinary results reported by Corning's Telecommunications Product Division:

- 24x decrease in product returns
- 10x improvement in on-time delivery

- Awarded the coveted Malcolm Baldridge National Quality Award in 1995 (Natitional Institute of Standards & Technology, 2001).

Once we started to understand the basic tenets underlying Goalsharing, we began to examine it more thoroughly so that we could take it to higher levels with our own clients.

Let's take a few moments to look at some of the more important things we've learned about this exciting management tool. Goalsharing is not a "program of the month." It is a proven process for helping organizations to not only survive, but also to thrive in a rapidly changing, highly competitive environment. In essence, Goalsharing is a means of working smart that engages and rewards employees for continuous improvement. Over time, it transitions employees to "business partners" and works extremely well in conjunction with Business Training.

Early Goalsharing pioneers recognized that employees: 1) have unique abilities, 2) prefer to understand and be involved in the business and 3) want to make a difference. They realized that, for employees to make their contribution, they needed to understand their business and have appropriate "line of sight" – to actually see how their efforts impact organizational results. Their organizations addressed this challenge by finding simple ways to communicate the goals of the business. They then helped staff members to see where they could make the biggest difference and taught them to craft simple goals that were specific, measurable and realistic, yet had a reasonable amount of "stretch." For some, their goals may have included metrics linked to revenue generation or cost containment. Others may have focused on goal areas such as operational effectiveness/ efficiency or customer satisfaction.

To improve synergy and minimize the likelihood of organizational conflict, these organizations ensured that department goals were: 1) aligned with a simple set of company financial and non-financial goals and 2) compatible across the organization. And to improve vertical alignment and employee line of sight, they encouraged supervisors to provide employees with the opportunity to propose their own goals. This approach went a long way toward improving motivation and mental ownership. Participating employees were then eligible for Goalsharing incentive payments linked to company financial performance, as well as individual and collective contributions against pre-determined goals.

To our surprise, some of the most impressive long-term results have occurred in large unionized companies facing difficult obstacles such as Corning, who pioneered the concept in 1989.

Over the last several years, we have had the opportunity to implement Goalsharing programs with many companies across industry. Our experience has taught us that small to large-sized clients alike, could realize significant results quickly, as demonstrated in one of our Goalsharing case studies below:

- A small construction services company had hit a wall. After launching one of our Goalsharing incentive programs, revenue and profit increased by more than 2X, and all within six months.

Our clients often ask us how long it should take before they see positive results from our Goalsharing incentive programs. We usually err on the conservative side by telling them that they can expect good results the first year, very good results the second year and excellent results from the third year on. Of course, when they are able to experience exceptional results in 3-6 months, that's very exciting!

While larger companies typically have more resources to draw upon in implementing a Goalsharing program, we usually find that Goalsharing is easier to implement in small to medium-sized organizations, and that the positive results tend to come within a much shorter timeframe.

Below are some basic guidelines to help you design your short-term incentive (Goalsharing) plan and get the biggest bang for the buck.

1. Decide what you want to achieve from your plan(s).

What are your organization's 5 – 7 most important financial and non-financial goals for the plan year? Have these goals been communicated in a way that your employees understand and appreciate? Is it clear what types of subordinate goals are needed to drive the accomplishment of your "big picture" goals? How can you get everyone aligned and going the same direction, while at the same time minimize the likelihood of goal conflict?

Once the organizational goals are selected and articulated, they need to be weighted within the organizational performance component of your incentive plan based on their relative importance. While there is no one size fits all approach, typically we find that each of these 5-7 organizational objectives should be weighted at least 10%. Often times revenue or profit is the most heavily weighted objective, but this varies by organization, and it is not out of line to weight some other objective most heavily.

2. Determine the appropriate relationship between organizational and departmental/ individual performance.

If rewards are based solely on organizational performance, what you have is a profit-sharing plan that may do little to incent your strongest performers. On the other hand, if payouts focus too much on individual/ department performance, you may fall short of achieving the desired synergy to become a healthy, high performance company. The key is achieving the right balance.

Accordingly, the second component of your organization's incentive plan would be individual/ departmental performance. This component of the plan allows each individual or department to key in on the aspects of their role that help the organization to achieve success. Additionally, this component provides the organization with a means of differentiating their star performers and rewarding them accordingly.

The most common approach here is to weight the organizational performance most heavily for executives, and to then develop a more balanced distribution of weightings as one works down the organizational hierarchy. The reason for this is that the executives are ultimately responsible for organizational performance, whereas lower level individuals have limited line of sight to organizational performance, but can certainly excel at achieving objectives relative to their position. As a starting point for discussion, you might consider a 70/30 (organizational/ individual performance) distribution for executives, a 60/30 distribution for managers & high-level professionals, and a 50/50 distribution for lower level professionals & nonexempt roles.

Quite often, determining the appropriate methodology for assessing individual performance can be the most challenging aspect of an effective incentive plan. We frequently suggest linking this component to a wholistic measure of individual performance, covering both the "what" & "how" components of performance. If your organization has a well-developed performance evaluation process that includes appropriate goal setting & cascading, then evaluation ratings may be a viable tie-in to your incentive plan. However, we typically find that existing performance appraisals are lacking. In such instances, we work with our clients to establish a goal-setting process for their employees (chapter 9) and/or work with them to re-vamp their performance evaluation process (chapter 11).

3. Determine eligibility requirements and pertinent provisions.

Who will be eligible to participate in the plan? How well do these employees understand your business? Do they see a clear relationship between their efforts and the bottom line? Have you addressed all related plan provisions? (For instance, how employees hired during the plan year will be treated). If such employees are to be included in the plan, how will they learn about plan goals and potential rewards? Also, how will you address employees who may be promoted, transferred or terminated mid-course?

Our clients typically include all full-time staff in their incentive plans. Doing so is the best way to create synergy throughout the organization. Typically, we suggest new hires must be on-board by no later than Oct. 1st (presuming a calendar year plan) in order to participate, and such participation would be on a pro-rata basis. Anything after Oct. 1st is usually too short of a time period to make any meaningful contribution towards the year's performance. However, in the instance of a highly sought-after executive you may be recruiting, there may need to be an exception or a hire-on incentive offered in lieu of waiting to participate until the following year.

4. Decide how payouts will be calculated and when these will be paid.

How should your short-term incentive plan fit into your total compensation strategy? How will you fund this program? What should annualized payout targets look like for each role? What should payouts look like under divergent company and individual performance scenarios? When will you pay any earned incentives? Annually? Semi-annually? Quarterly?

The approach we typically recommend to our clients is a target incentive methodology for their executives. Such an approach will express targeted incentive as a percentage of base salary (i.e. 25%). Utilizing this approach provides executives with a tangible incentive target that can easily fit into the overall compensation strategy. To determine an appropriate incentive target, survey data should be considered, and an appropriate incentive should be arrived upon in accordance with the company's total compensation philosophy, while considering the mix of compensation components offered.

Organizations then need to consider developing pay-for-performance metrics surrounding their organizational & individual performance objectives. Of course, attainment of a goal would render an incentive payout equal to 100% of the weighted incentive target. However, the big question is what to do if performance is somewhat above or below expectations? This is where pay-for-performance metrics fill in the gaps. We recommend our clients consider at least 2 other performance levels in addition to target for each objective:

- Threshold performance - threshold represents the bare minimum acceptable level of performance in order to warrant any level of incentive. While each organization is unique, a reasonable starting point for discussion is to consider 80-90% of target performance for the objective and/or performance that is typically equal to or slightly greater than the prior year and attainable with roughly 80% certainty. In regard to incentive earnings, threshold incentive payments are typically in the range of 30-50% of the weighted target incentive.

- Superior performance - superior represents significant overachievement that is at the very top end of realistic performance expectations. As with thresholds, superior performance is unique to each organization, but something in the neighborhood of 120-130% of target performance tends to be a common starting point for discussion. We often suggest that superior performance should be only attainable with 10% certainty. In regard to incentive earnings, superior level incentive payments are typically in the range of 150-200% of the weighted target incentive. Generally, the larger the organization, the more likely they are to offer 200% leverage for superior performance. Most of our mid-size privately-held organizations tend to offer 150% leverage for superior performance.

Once target, threshold, and superior are defined for each performance objective, the rest is somewhat mechanical. Companies can either build in a few more steps to bridge the gaps, or they can specify that performance between the 3 categories is addressed on a straight-line basis.

In regard to frequency of incentives, annual plans are by far the most common. Annual plans are easiest to administer and focus the team on the attainment of year-end performance outcomes. However, annual plans can at times be less engaging for participants. Accordingly, a number of our clients are looking for semi-annual or quarterly plans. These plans can be more engaging, but do have more design complexities and are more administratively burdensome.

5. Decide what type of training and communications are needed to implement your program effectively.

Remember, a good plan implemented well, is better than an excellent plan implemented poorly. (Of course, you will want your plan to be designed AND implemented well!)

Research indicates that many organizations put a good bit of thought into designing their incentive plans. Unfortunately, many fall short during the roll-out. Communication is critical here. To be effective, your managers needs to understand and fully support your incentive program. They, as well as their employees, must be clear about the workings of these programs, their respective responsibilities, and what each participant must focus on to achieve the desired results.

As you can see, properly designed incentive programs can yield tremendous benefits to your organization and your employees. Yet, more often than not, these plans are met with resistance. Some managers and non-management employees may resist personal accountability. Others may resist change. However, we all understand the now famous expression: "Change or Die!" Make sure you are prepared for some level of resistance and stay the course.

It is best to involve your managers and employees early in the process and to introduce these plans carefully. Since we are all creatures of habit, it is important to hold each other accountable for the success of your program. Ongoing communication is key. Some companies find it beneficial to utilize their quarterly "all hands" meetings as an opportunity to share progress to date, celebrate successes, and brainstorm ideas for getting back (or staying) on track. Of course, every organization is different, so it's important to customize your program to the needs of your company. Too much is at stake here, and you do not want this to end up being just another "program of the month!"

Once you start seeing positive results, you will probably ask yourself why you didn't implement such a plan sooner!

" A well-structured incentive program can boost productivity and instill a sense of shared responsibility among employees; a haphazardly designed program, on the other hand, can make a bad problem even worse." Michael Alter

Chapter 8

Retaining Your Top Performers
(Long-Term Incentives)

There's a wonderful global organization called Vistage, which helps private company CEOs and business owners take their companies to the next level (www.vistage.com). Member companies of this CEO Forum range from <$5 million to over $50 million in annual revenue.

With small organizations like these fueling the U.S. economy, Vistage members are continuously on the lookout for creative ways to gain and sustain a competitive advantage in the marketplace.

Over the last several years, we have been fortunate to work with dozens of Vistage members throughout Southern California, as well as several other areas of the country. This experience has taught us a great deal about the entrepreneurial mindset, as well as the challenges these executives face.

One day, we received an intriguing call from one of the local Vistage Chairs. He had just finished facilitating one of his group meetings and mentioned we would be hearing from a few of his members. The Chair went on to explain that the group's meeting had focused on the controversial topic of whether or not private company owners should grant equity to their key leaders. Apparently, the discussion went back and forth and, at one point, got pretty intense. After the Chair allowed the discussion to proceed for quite a while, he wrapped it up by suggesting that they call LTC Performance Strategies. Two members called us the next day.

By the way, the answer to the above question as to whether private companies should grant equity is: "It depends." Let's look at a couple of case studies:

Case of the (Regrettably) Generous Business Owner

A few years back, we received an invitation to meet with the owner of an incredibly successful private company. We were forewarned that he was absolutely brilliant and could be quite challenging. When we met with the owner, he was everything we expected. We listened in awe as he shared his company's amazing story.

The owner's purpose in meeting with us was to better understand how executive compensation could be designed to improve executive retention. You see, the CEO who had worked for him for several years, abruptly resigned. As the proud business owner recounted the story, we detected a degree of vulnerability, as well as genuine sadness and extreme disappointment.

The owner had provided the CEO with a competitive salary and some incredibly generous annual bonuses (several million dollars, during this last economic recession). Surely, the CEO would have felt eternally grateful and worked for the business owner for many, many years, wouldn't he? Well, apparently not. One day, the CEO walked into the owner's office and dropped the bomb. Apparently, he had always dreamed about traveling around the world and now he had the financial resources to do so.

The CEO's resignation hit the owner like a ton of bricks and he became determined to never let this happen again. This experience taught him a valuable lesson about the importance of having a more intelligently designed and balanced compensation program.

Fast forward… the owner hired a new CEO with a very differently structured compensation package. It consists of a reasonable salary, a much more conservative, (yet market-based) short-term incentive plan, and an attractive (non-equity based) long-term incentive (retention) plan. The newly hired CEO realizes that if he decides to "walk," he will be leaving a good bit of money on the table.

By the way, the owner also began looking at offering the new CEO participation in a nonqualified deferred compensation program, which would allow him to voluntarily defer annual earnings (tax play) and let his earnings grow tax deferred. This Plan would also offer the Company some very attractive financial benefits. (Executive deferral plans are covered in Chapter 10).

Case of the Prudent Owner and a Win-Win Transition

Let's now look at a second case that involves another privately-owned company. Below are some considerations that made this case particularly interesting:

- *The 100% owner informed his leadership team, cautiously and confidentially, of his interest in putting the Company up for sale; he realized, of course, that executive retention would be critically important to any prospective buyer.*

- *The team members expressed a willingness to remain with the organization, with the understanding that they would participate in a long-term compensation plan.*

- *The CEO (and his team members) realized that, because of existing environmental issues, the Company might not be salable.*

- *Some of the team members realized that if the company was to sell to a larger organization, their role might be duplicative, and because of this, they might not be needed by the acquiring company.*

- The owner had heard horror stories from companies who had granted real equity, so this consideration was off the table. However, he agreed to share a certain percentage of any net proceeds from the sale of the company with his executive team.

- The owner was concerned about being locked into granting certain payout percentages to each of his team members, realizing that the personal performance of his executive team members might fluctuate from year to year.

In an effort to meet the divergent needs of the various stakeholders, we developed 2 distinct, but integrated, long-term compensation plans that were flexible enough to reward the desired performance and outcomes, without allowing the executives to "double dip" on these plans:

- A 3-year Long-Term Incentive Plan (LTIP) providing an attractive cash reward linked to company and participant performance. Participants could qualify for a reward under this Plan if the Company met its performance goals, but didn't sell before the end of this 3-year performance period. It addressed the needs of those individuals who, while skeptical about if and when the company might sell, were willing to remain with the company for the defined performance period.

- A more lucrative "Net Proceeds" Plan whereby team members could receive a share of the Net Proceeds derived from a Change of Control for remaining up to and through the course of an ownership transition.

To prevent the likelihood of double dipping, we incorporated a provision that, if the Company sold following the payout of the 3-year cash-based LTIP, then any proceeds from the LTIP would simply be subtracted from the more lucrative Net Proceeds Plan.

Oh yes, to minimize the likelihood of executive team members "slacking off", we also incorporated a provision that would allow the

COO to adjust participant payout percentages to better link rewards to individual performance/ contributions.

As it turned out, the Company was successfully sold before the end of the LTIP performance period. The executive participants were paid out in accordance with the Net Proceeds Plan provisions; some were asked to stay on with the new owner; others parted amicably, with cash in hand.

So as you can see, the question really isn't whether to give equity or not, but whether to offer a long-term compensation program, and if so, in what form. So that leads to the question: "what is the purpose of long-term compensation?"

The primary purpose of long-term compensation should be to attract, retain and build ownership among key executives, while focusing them on performance factors that will drive long-term profitable growth, enterprise value, and shareholder return. The full-value of any such reward should not be 100% realizable until at least several years from the date of grant, thus making it "long-term." Long-term compensation can be one of a company's most significant investments, as these plans can, at times, represent a sizeable portion of an executive's total compensation.

So with such an emphasis being placed on getting long-term compensation right- both in terms of driving performance and retention-where does one begin?

Prevalence

According to a recent World at Work Survey (WorldatWork, 2016), the majority of privately-held companies surveyed offer some form of long-term compensation. In this survey, 53% of private company respondents reported having long-term compensation for their executives. Comparatively, close to

100% of publicly traded companies offer long-term compensation.

Determine Eligibility

Companies offering long-term compensation must determine who will be eligible to participate in the long-term compensation plan. Typically, all of those individuals on the Executive Team would be included in such a plan. In essence, what it really comes down to is, who are the company's key strategic leaders that are best positioned to make a significant impact on the long-term performance and value of the company? Another question a company should consider: whose departure could deliver a major blow to the organization?

Remember a good long-term compensation plan should drive performance and support retention of key individuals!

Determine Target Values

In the earlier chapters we discussed the topic of determining a company's compensation positioning philosophy and mix of salary, short-term and long-term incentives. As with salary & short-term incentive data, benchmarking the external market is a solid foundational approach in determining an appropriate target value for long-term compensation. This said, however, benchmarking long-term compensation in private companies can be very challenging, as practices vary greatly and long-term compensation does not necessarily exist in all privately-held organizations. A trusted advisor can be very useful in helping you to determine appropriate long-term compensation target values.

The most common way for long-term compensation to be expressed is by utilizing the term "multiples." A multiple is simply one's long-term incentive target in relation to salary. For example, a multiple of 1.5x would indicate that the long-term incentive target is one and a half times salary. Since long-term compensation plans should, by definition, be longer than one year, the multiple is typically expressed in terms of the annualized value of the incentive. An alternative approach is to reference long-term compensation in terms of percentage of company equity/ value (i.e. 5% or 5% of the growth).

Determine the Appropriate Plan Vehicle

There are many forms of long-term compensation vehicles that a company could consider utilizing for their plan. These plans include, but are not limited to: incentive stock options, nonqualified stock options, time-based restricted stock, performance-based restricted stock, phantom stock and long-term cash incentives. All of these plans carry their own unique pros and cons and their applicability will vary based on the unique circumstances of each situation.

It is important to note that none of these plans necessarily needs to be utilized in isolation. It is, in fact, quite common for a company to utilize an omnibus incentive plan that authorizes the usage of any of the above vehicles, at any time, as part of their long-term incentive and retention strategy. This methodology is often referred to as the "portfolio approach." Below is a summary of each of the most prevalent vehicle choices:

Equity Based Plans

- *Restricted Stock* - A plan where an executive is granted shares of stock that are subject to forfeiture unless certain conditions (restrictions) are met. These restrictions could either be time-based or performance-based (commonly called "Performance Shares"). An example of a time-based restriction would be having to remain with the company for five years. An example of a performance-based restriction would be having stock linked to achieving a pre-determined, 3-year EPS (earnings per share) goal.

Performance Shares are becoming a more commonly utilized form of equity-based long-term compensation. Performance based equity vehicles were reported to be utilized by 17% of long-term granting privately held organizations, per World at Work (World at Work, 2016). Time-based shares continue to be utilized in certain circumstances, such as when a company may need to recruit a top-notch executive away from a competitor in which the departing executive would be leaving a good bit of money on the table. In the same World at Work Survey, time-based equity was reported to be utilized by 22% of long-term granting privately held organizations.

The advantage of restricted stock is that it turns executives into owners, thus aligning their interests with that of the owners. Restricted stock also encourages retention, since an executive would be forgoing the value if they left prior to the end of the restriction period. Performance-shares have gained the most traction lately, because in addition to the above-mentioned advantages, these shares also have the ability to strongly link pay to performance.

A disadvantage of restricted stock is that it dilutes existing shareholders by issuing additional shares for which no purchase price was paid. Time-based shares are also criticized as being a "freebie" because they lack a pay for performance relationship outside of share price. In private companies, equity- based plans are often shied away from because the process of valuing a private company can be burdensome and expensive. Additionally, granting equity means bringing in new business partners who will carry voting rights, unless otherwise specified.

Restricted stock is expensed over the restriction period at fair market value at the time of grant. The gain is taxed to the executive as ordinary income at the time of restriction lapse. The executive does have the option to make an IRS 83b election and pay taxes at the time of grant, on what is presumably (or hopefully) a lesser value than at the time restrictions lapse. Taxation of performance shares is somewhat dependent upon the nature of the specific plan design.

- **Stock Options** - A plan that grants an executive the right to purchase a fixed number of shares of company common stock at a fixed price over a specified period of time.

In the past, Stock Options were a very widely utilized form of long-term compensation, but their usage has been declining every year due to changes in accounting and tax treatment and lack of pay for performance relationship. According to the 2016 World at Work Survey of Private Companies, stock options are offered by 30% of long-term granting organizations.

One advantage of utilizing stock options is that the design of these plans can be very flexible. Additionally, because executives must invest their personal money, they have a vested interest as owners.

One of the disadvantages is that options are taxed when exercised, so there is no tax deferral. This is burdensome for an executive who must have the money to exercise the options and pay the taxes as well. Options have also been criticized for encouraging risky executive behavior, in an effort to drive up stock prices with little regard for the downside. Additionally, options have no linkage to performance, outside of share price. In private companies, equity-based plans are often avoided because valuing a private company can be a burdensome and expensive endeavor. Finally, granting equity means bringing in new business partners who will carry voting rights, unless otherwise specified.

Options are expensed over the vesting period at fair market value at the time of grant. The gain is taxed to the executive as ordinary income at the time of exercise.

Most stock options (those described above) are considered Nonqualified. An alternate variation, Incentive Stock Options, has more plan design restrictions, but allows for capital gains tax treatment rather than ordinary income.

Phantom Equity Based Plans

- ***Phantom Stock*** – These plans can be designed in a variety of ways to mirror the value of equity-based plans, without the complications of using real equity. So, rather than granting actual shares, awards represent a promise to pay the employee the equivalent cash value of the shares at some point in the future.

These plans are useful in situations where companies do not want, or cannot have, employees owning actual shares, but want to share equity-like value. Since these plans do not issue actual shares, shareholder equity is not diluted. As such, these types of plans are very popular with our privately-held clients. According to the 2016 World at Work Survey of privately-held organizations, 23% of long-term granting organizations utilize some form of phantom stock.

A disadvantage is that Phantom Stock Plans, like equity plans, are linked to company value, which isn't necessarily the only indicator of company performance. However, performance measures could be incorporated into such a plan in order to either determine vesting, granting and/or actualized earnings. These plans can, at times, be more difficult to communicate to employees who are skeptical of a plan that doesn't grant them real equity.

One of the most popular versions of a Phantom Stock Plan is what we have coined a "Net Proceeds Plan." This type of plan delivers the majority of its value to the executive(s) if a change of control occurs during their employment, which is, of course, the "big ticket" event for many private company owners.

- *Nonqualified Stock Alternative Plan* - A flexible deferred compensation plan that, like a phantom stock plan, can be developed to mirror an equity -based plan, but with several tax and other advantages to the organization and participants. The greatest advantage is no company stock dilution for the current shareholders, while still providing participants with true secondary investments.

Cash Based Long-Term Plans

- *Performance Award (Long-Term Incentive Plan)* - Performance awards are essentially incentive plans tied to performance of ≥1 year and designed to pay out over multiple years. Performance awards can be linked to a number of measures such as improvement in share price, earnings before interest, tax, depreciation and amortization (EBITDA), sales, and quality.

Performance awards are becoming increasingly prevalent in both private and public companies alike. They can be utilized as a sole long-term plan or coupled with an equity (or phantom equity) plan.

These plans are advantageous because of their simplicity and the fact that they can directly link pay to performance. These plans are attractive because they are infinitely flexible in design and can be settled in cash. In addition, these plans do not dilute shareholder equity. In the 2016 World at Work survey, long-term cash plans were by far the most favored vehicle, with 44% of long-term granting privately-held organizations reporting offering such plans.

Performance awards are sometimes criticized because: (1) they do not provide executives with a true ownership stake, and (2) it is sometimes difficult to establish accurate long-term goals.

The estimated value of such plans should be accrued over the performance period. Any payout is taxable to the executive as ordinary income when vested and paid. Alternatively, payouts could be placed into a nonqualified deferral plan in order to offset the current tax implications.

- ***Executive 162 "Stay" Bonus*** - A tax-advantaged plan that incents executive retention. The annual bonus amount is paid into a Tier One corporate-owned life insurance (COLI) policy. The employer has a great deal of flexibility in designing these plans and may tie bonuses to performance and/or the company's stock appreciation.

While the above list offers you a number of choices, there are others, as well. The plan you select should address your unique circumstances. A careful analysis conducted by a skilled executive compensation consultant should help you to arrive at your optimal plan.

At this point you will want to begin to consider the following topics as you move forward:

1) **Eligibility.** Who are your key strategic leaders whom you need to retain and motivate to drive long-term performance and value?

2) **Payout "Multiples" (Targets).** What is a competitive long-term incentive target for the attainment of reasonable "stretch" performance? How does this fit in with your current offerings and total compensation strategy?

3) **Delivery Vehicles.** What makes the most sense for your particular scenario: equity, phantom equity, cash, etc.? Should you be confined to one vehicle or should you take a "portfolio" approach?

4) **Payout Metrics for Various Levels of Performance.** What will constitute threshold, target and superior performance? What will be the payouts associated with such levels of performance?

5) **Performance Measurements (Goals).** Based on the plan you have chosen, what will performance be tied to? If utilizing multiple goals, how will they be weighted?

6) **Performance Period Length.** What constitutes a reasonable long-term horizon in your business? Keep in mind that if the timeframe is too short, you're basically offering a second short-term incentive and doing little to retain your executives or drive long-term performance. However, if the horizon is too long, the incentive may lose some of its potency and fail to drive the desired performance and behavior. We find the most common performance period is 3 – 4 years.

7) **Frequency of New Plans.** Will plans be "rolling," such that a new plan begins each year and overlaps with earlier plans? Or will a new plan only begin once the previous cycle has been completed?

8) **Vesting.** Once the performance period has ended and the payout determined, will it be paid out all at once or paid out over a period of time?

9) **Provisions.** What other provisions and contingencies must be addressed before developing all plan documents and communications?

Remember, your Long-term Incentive Plan needs to be aligned with your company's strategic plan and associated goals. The plan needs to be designed carefully, as long-term compensation can potentially represent the largest portion of an executive's total compensation "mix." While the company's short-term incentive plan may be a company's most potent vehicle for driving short-term performance and behavior, the long-term incentive plan may be the most potent vehicle for driving long-term performance and value, and retaining the key executives charged with doing so.

A well-designed Long-Term Incentive Plan should communicate:

- Where the company is going (vision)
- How it is going to get there (strategy/ key initiatives)
- What it needs key people to do (roles, goals and expectations)
- How it will reward that effort (incentives)

Now, you may be thinking that this is all fine and well, but I'm not sure that I need to offer my executives a long-term plan, and maybe I don't want to. Again, there is nothing that says private company CEOs or business owners need to offer such a plan. However, the job market has rebounded from our recent recession, and you may wish to ensure that your total rewards program is still attractive and competitive.

According to a May 2013 survey by OI Partners, 70% of the respondents stated that retaining talent was their greatest challenge. In fact, 51% of the surveyed companies indicated that they were experiencing greater turnover in 2013, across all organizational levels, and 75% are anticipating further turnover. Below are a couple of excerpts from this study:

- 34% indicate higher turnover among "high potentials"
- 29% stated that they had lost more senior level talent than the previous year
- 27% experienced higher turnover in the middle management ranks (Hollon, 2013)

Study participants were especially concerned about losing "high potentials" and mid-level managers who are viewed as the future leaders of their companies.

Bear in mind that offering a long-term compensation plan need not represent an expensive endeavor; in fact, the plan can be designed to be self-funded and should provide a solid return on investment (ROI).

When headhunters will inevitably try to recruit some of your key executives, you may wish to make it more difficult for them to do so. If all they feel they have to do is offer a higher salary or bonus value, that may not prove to be too difficult in today's market. But if your executives understand that they may need to walk away from a good chunk of change, this will make it less likely for them to jump at the first chance.

Chapter 9

Selecting and Aligning Your Performance Goals

Over the years, many organizations have made progress in their efforts to link pay to performance. In fact, a number of these have developed clear-cut performance metrics and associated payout formulas. These efforts have helped them to achieve a better return on investment (ROI) from their executive compensation programs.

Despite these advances, we have found that most companies suffer from the same weakness and that is the inability to properly select and align the right goals throughout the organization. Interestingly, many of these same organizations have taken pain-staking efforts to ensure that their employees understand how to write SMART goals. (That is goals that are Specific, Measurable, Action-Oriented, Realistic and Time Sensitive). However, most of the C-level executives we have worked with struggle in selecting the right top-level organizational goals. And, of course, if senior management doesn't select the proper goals at the top of the organization and ensure that these goals are compatible, then conflicts will materialize, motivation will suffer, and the company will fail to achieve the desired synergy and results. This, quite frankly, has been the reason so many MBO (Management by Objectives) programs have failed and ultimately gone by the wayside.

While many of our clients have asked us to teach their managers and employees how to properly articulate their performance goals, more and more have invited us to provide training on selecting the right goals. These latter efforts have been extremely well received with proven short and long-term results.

So, as we've searched for and tried to share best practices, we have found that a significant and growing number of leading companies are not only extremely goal-oriented, but have also become quite skilled at selecting and articulating the right-top tier goals, and then aligning them up, down, and across their organizations.

Many leaders of less successful organizations think about goals just as often, but fail in their efforts to create a synergistic, goal-based culture. Since this topic is so important, we've provided the following table to guide you in your efforts here:

Criteria	Less Effective Organizations	More Effective Organizations
Number of Top-Tier Goals	Too few or too many goals	5 – 7 clear cut goals
Balance	Top-tier goals are strictly financial	Goals are balanced (include both financial and non-financial criteria)
Clarity	Goals are "fuzzy" (hard to measure/ ensure the proper focus for both team and individual efforts)	Goals are SMART (specific, measurable, action-oriented, realistic and time-sensitive)
Compatibility Between Departments	Department goals conflict with one another (e.g. sales vs. operations)	Goals are carefully established to create win-win scenarios across department lines
Engagement/ Ownership	Employees are given "their" goals	Employees draft personal goals after reviewing those of their supervisors
Alignment	Goals are poorly aligned and ineffective	Each employee's goals support higher level supervisory/ organizational goals
Communication	Goals are formally discussed 1-2 times per year; yet real accomplishments are hard to assess at year-end	Employees brief supervisors on goal progress on a regular basis; supervisors become coaches in helping their employees to succeed
Motivation	Goals process breaks down; initiative becomes another "program of the month"	Employees become engaged, proactive and flexible; goal focus spills over into other areas of their lives
Long-Term Effectiveness	Supervisors/ employees resort to old habits	First year results tend to be good; results improve each year as new habits are ingrained

So when you decide to implement or update your organization's incentive program(s), don't forget effective goal setting. Selecting, articulating and aligning the right goals will allow your organization to achieve the greatest return on investment from its incentive plans.

Chapter 10

Getting Even More from Your Incentive Plans

One of our favorite stories deals with one of America's most successful companies. What makes this story particularly intriguing is that the company almost went bankrupt!

An American Success Story: SRC

Back in the early 80's, Springfield Remanufacturing Company (SRC) spun off from International Harvester. SRC remanufactures heavy-duty engines; a very messy business. The company was failing, and employee morale had taken a toll. Most of the employees didn't feel too good about management and the feelings seemed mutual.

Nearing the brink of disaster, SRC's Chief Executive, Jack Stack, brought the troops together and offered them the following deal: He would teach them the business and if they could turn things around, they'd all share in the management bonus.

What happened was nothing short of a miracle. Not only did the company survive, but it became an American icon. The company's revenue climbed from $16M to over $400M and the stock price soared from 10 cents to $134 per share…that's right- from 10 cents to $134 per share!!! And during this time, SRC has spun off 17 companies (Wikipedia).

Jack knew that the purpose of the business was to generate cash for the owners, and if the employees were to ever think like owners, they needed to understand the business, including the numbers behind their own business. Jack was credited with coining the term "Open Book Management," which involves sharing company financials with employees. He also began preaching about the importance of Business Education. Open Book Management immediately began drawing the attention of the media and the company began holding onsite conferences and sharing their approach to Open Book Management with other forward-thinking companies. LTC Owners Terry and Larry Comp were among thousands of business executives and owners who traveled to SRC. During their respective trips, Terry and Larry had an opportunity to meet hourly employees who had risen through the ranks and been given the opportunity to run some of the company's spin offs. Terry developed a passion for teaching employees business fundamentals and became one of the recognized pioneers within the field of "Business Literacy."

You may be wondering why we began this chapter with this story. Well, one day as we were looking back at the many opportunities we've had to help our clients in developing their incentive compensation plans, we came to a startling realization: our greatest success stories had one thing in common- a secret success ingredient. The "secret sauce" was that in each of these client engagements, we had been asked to first teach their employees the basics of business and the fundamentals of their own business.

Here's an important realization that we've had- many employees welcome this type of information. At their core, most are looking for an opportunity to make a difference…to make their contribution. Below is one of our case studies that illustrates how business training can engage and motivate the troops, while making a big difference to the bottom line.

The Case of the Empowered Workforce

Several years ago we were chatting with the CEO of a $25M (revenue) services company. During our conversation, he expressed frustration with the lack of employee engagement and the sense of entitlement he felt permeated his organization. The CEO had ambitious goals for his company, but it was just "humming" along (Think ho-hum). He had recently learned about the benefits of teaching business essentials to employees and knew that one of our *partners was a pioneer in the area of Open Book Management and teaching the essentials of business.*

Soon, the CEO invited us to teach business fundamentals to his employees with a specific focus on THEIR business. In no time, it became apparent that they were hungry for this type of training and soon began to connect the dots. It was great to witness morale improving, as well as the business gaining traction.

Unfortunately, bad things happen. The company lost its biggest client, which accounted for roughly 1/3 of its business. Immediately, the executive team began meeting behind closed doors, in an effort to keep the news quiet, while they figured out how to solve the problem. Budgets were immediately cut to the bone. Shortly thereafter, employee morale and trust levels sank to a new low.

When we followed up with the CEO, we asked if he had involved the troops in identifying cost savings. (After all, they had just completed a series of business classes and might be able to help). To make a long story short, he strongly doubted whether the employees would be able to do so, but agreed to let us design a 60-day "Gainsharing" Program. As part of this initiative, the employees were asked to nominate a team of their peers who would review cost savings suggestions and determine which were legitimate. To add some flavor to the program, we asked the employees to come up with a theme, which they did: "Show Me the Money!"

Prior to the launch, the CEO reiterated that his management team had racked their brains and insisted there were NO more cost savings to be found. Yet, within a matter of weeks, the employees of this small private company uncovered over $300,000 in "hidden" savings!" Perhaps, none of us should have been surprised. After all, the employees were closest to the customers, had been trained to better understand their business, and had a chance to show off their stuff.

Soon afterward, we got a call from the company's HR Director informing us that the CEO was walking around "like Santa Claus", delivering Gainsharing checks. In retrospect, the money seemed far less important to the employees than the pride they realized from helping their company get back on track.

We all know that money has the power to motivate and you may be thinking that money may have been a significant factor in this story. Interestingly, the Goalsharing payouts were quite modest, so in this case, the real motivation was apparently something less concrete. But let's look at another case study that makes this point even more definitively:

The Case of the OTD Turn-Around

A local manufacturing company had also become intrigued with the concept of Open Book Management and teaching Business Essentials. They invited us to teach a series of short business classes to their management and professional staff. The training was a big hit and we were subsequently invited to roll out the same type of training to their production folks. This group was even more fun to teach, and it was gratifying to see the light bulbs come on.

Immediately after the training, the Company's Chair invited us to help the Company tackle its biggest problem: On Time Delivery. When we asked him what the OTD % was, the Chair's face turned beet red. He admitted that the company had no idea, and then mentioned that he would be eternally grateful if we could: (1) help them identify their true metrics, and (2) provide them with an understanding of how to improve OTD performance, as this problem was causing them to lose some of their biggest clients.

Within a short time, we discovered that their OTD was 77%, meaning that 23% of orders weren't reaching their clients on time. We ended up facilitating a few meetings with a small cross section of the new "Business Essentials" graduates. Within 2 months, OTD climbed from 77% to 94%...and by the end of the year, reached 98%...we were excited to see the troops turn the company's biggest weakness into its most significant strength...all within a matter of a few months.

Oh yes, there was no monetary incentive tied to this critical business initiative.

So, it's not difficult to understand why Business Essentials training is such a potent tool. We ask employees to set goals and we tend to be disappointed with the outcome. It's no wonder... if they don't understand the business, how can they know what the key problems are, and where to focus their energies?

Taking some time to teach employees the basics of your business conveys a level of respect and sends a message that "we're all in this together and we need your help."

So when you're looking to get an even bigger "bang for the buck" on your short and long-term incentive plans, consider carving out a bit of time to help your employees to help you.

Chapter 11

Managing Performance

Student: *"Teacher, how would you define the state of performance appraisal in today's organization?"*

Teacher: *"That human encounter which keeps the manager awake the night before and the employee the night after."*

Wow…while the above dialog is meant to be humorous, it creates quite a picture, huh?

When I (Larry) got my first corporate job, I recall doing some extensive research on performance appraisal. The findings were quite controversial, but largely disappointing. Now, some 30+ years later, it seems in some ways that not much has changed. Sure, we now have robust software packages that allow us to fill out our appraisal forms online and view colorful charts and graphs to compare and contrast team members' performance and identify trends. But… let's get real! There is no automated product that replaces building and maintaining a relationship of trust with the people you lead. Yes, 360-degree feedback can be meaningful and helpful, and those systems can improve a manager's efficiency and save time. But, without frequent feedback/ dialogue and agreed-upon goals, and absent a real relationship and a culture of accountability, the best software in the world will **never** move the needle, No matter how advanced our technology becomes, you cannot automate (or outsource) the kind of leadership that creates an environment where people feel respected, challenged to do their best work, and supported in their personal and professional development goals.

So Change is Needed....Is it Working Now?

In fairness, some organizations have worked tirelessly in recent years to identify improvements needed in the review process and re-engineer their systems. A year or two after the changes, a few notable organizations point to (somewhat) increased satisfaction with the performance management process on the part of employees and managers. Yet most of the evidence suggests that while some issues may have been addressed and corrected, new concerns have arisen in the process., and the net/net, in many cases, is a wash at best. Perhaps the real issue is that performance management is not about the perfect form, automated or otherwise. Effective performance management and development is only achieved in the context of a culture where people are: encouraged and supported by their manager; assisted in setting and achieving meaningful goals; provided with frequent feedback; held accountable for results, and rewarded accordingly. In other words, great leaders integrate these vital practices into their daily efforts, and it makes a significant difference in the improvement and development of individual performance. And, of course, when individual performance improves, organizational performance gains follow. Research tells us that top performing organizations create the cultures that support this kind of great leadership, while focusing their individual efforts on developing the fullest potential of their people.

So- since pay for performance is our topic at hand, how can you have a strong compensation or rewards program without a strong performance development system?

Performance Development vs. Appraisal

For many years, the annual event described in the anecdote at the beginning of this chapter has been essentially "a look in the rearview mirror"- a performance appraisal performed by the manager for a one-way conversation at year end with his/her team member. Clearly, the world we live in is different, and the changes we have experienced in the employer-employee relationship need to be reflected in the system we use to measure and develop each individual's performance. Organizations that implement more progressive approaches to managing performance, while holding people accountable, recognize and attempt to address the following employee needs: (1) a clear sense of direction; an understanding of *why* they do *what* they do, and how their job makes a difference (2) an opportunity to participate in setting goals and clarifying expectations; (3) timely, frequent, honest and meaningful feedback/dialogue on their performance; (4) consistency in how they are treated compared to others; and (5) support in achieving their business and career development goals. Most importantly, these more progressive systems rely upon the premise that performance development is an ongoing process, not an annual event. It is integrated into the life of the organization and becomes a hallmark of their culture.

Top Ten Principles

To get the best results from your performance development process, keep these "top ten" principles in mind:

1. Integrate/ align the performance management system with the desired organizational culture.

2. Demonstrate management support for the program. (If executives don't model it, others will not buy-in to the process).

3. Shift focus, understanding, and *practice* from a past, behaviorally-oriented annual EVENT to a future, goal-oriented, continuous PROCESS.

4. Align goals horizontally as well as vertically throughout the organization, and ensure employee-manager collaboration in setting goals.

5. Make sure to measure/evaluate both the WHAT and HOW of performance- the results and the manner in which they are accomplished.

6. Make the process administratively simple. (If managers don't do it, it can't possibly be effective!)

7. Determine how to appropriately link pay to performance. (If top, average, and poor performers receive equal treatment in terms of rewards, what is the message to the team?)

8. Incorporate ongoing, frequent feedback to build trust, correct any misunderstandings, and ensure there are no surprises. We recommend brief (at least quarterly) touch-base meetings that are documented.

9. Train managers and communicate, communicate, communicate their roles and responsibilities. (The best program poorly communicated is worse than a mediocre one that is well understood).

10. Recognize that positive culture change doesn't happen overnight; walk before you run.

Building a progressive performance development system around these 10 principles should help you and your staff to achieve a strong pay for performance compensation program, while helping your team members achieve their best and highest potential. It should also help everyone get a good night's sleep, even during the formal review season!

Chapter 12

Helping Your Executives to Build Capital for the Future

Several years ago, we received an urgent call from a close professional colleague, the Vice President of Human Resources for a local hi-tech company. He asked if I (Larry) could meet with he and his CFO ASAP. The next day we met for lunch and the two executives explained their dilemma. Their company had implemented an ineffective long-term capital accumulation plan that had totally bombed. The problem, they explained, was that nobody understood the plan. And, of course, if nobody understands the plan, then it can't serve as an effective motivational or retention tool. To top it off, the company's CEO was on a rampage and wanted this problem dealt with immediately!

Fortunately, we were able to get our Executive Benefits partner who had designed our own company's executive deferral plan to fly in and examine the plan with us. After facilitating a brief educational overview of plan considerations and design alternatives, he uncovered a number of deficiencies in the existing plan. He then provided a simple roadmap to solving our colleague's problem, and began working with us to draft a non-qualified deferred compensation (NQDC) plan that was customized to the needs of the executive participants, as well as the company. The plan was subsequently approved and became a big hit. Since then, the NQDC plan has expanded from 4 to over 35 participants and grown to more than $25M in assets. It has been extremely well received and has served as an exceptional tool for attracting and retaining executive talent, while allowing participants to build serious capital for the future.

You may find that an Executive Deferral Plan offers some significant advantages to your key executives, while also helping you to build your Balance Sheet. Let's first zero in on Nonqualified Deferred Compensation Plans (NQDC) as a plan design alternative.

Nonqualified Deferred Compensation Programs are not subject to the same set of ERISA laws governing qualified plans, such as 401(k) plans. NQDCs are not appropriate for each and every private company. However, they offer several distinct and attractive features such as:

- Companies (not the government) determine plan eligibility
- Eligible participants can defer whatever percentage of income (salary, bonus, long-term compensation) the company allows
- Executives defer current taxes while compounding tax-deferred earnings
- Investment choices can mirror those provided in a 401(k) Plan
- Participants can set up special "in-service" accounts which allow them to take monetary distributions early, without penalty
- Participants don't pay income tax until they receive distributions from their deferred compensation plan
- Companies can choose from among several funding vehicles (e.g. Corporate Owned Life Insurance, mutual funds)
- Plans allow the Company to build an asset, thereby strengthening its Balance Sheet
- Plans can be designed to parallel a company's time horizon (i.e. planned change of control) and pay for-performance philosophy
- Plans are inexpensive to administer and can be structured to provide cost recovery
- Emergency distributions may be possible in the case of certain types of unforeseen financial hardships
- Plans can serve as an exceptional recruitment and retention vehicle. Remember, a company's greatest expense is its investment in top people. Top companies use these plans to recruit and retain top talent

However, there are some additional factors to consider:

- Participant balances are subject to the claims of creditors of the corporation in the event of bankruptcy
- The corporation forgoes the immediate tax deduction on the deferred compensation. The good news is that the company will typically have a much larger deduction, later, when benefits are paid

A note of caution at this point. While there is no shortage of qualified plan (i.e. 401k) providers, there are relatively few non-qualified plan providers who understand the intimate details surrounding NQDC plans. This makes it difficult for most of us to be able to objectively evaluate alternative plan designs, product providers and plan administrators.

Our executive benefits partner realized the above dilemma. A few years after we introduced him to the client mentioned above, he went on to co-create a patented software program that examines over 200 points of differentiation to help interested companies objectively select the optimal product design, provider and plan administrator. Over the last few years, many of our clients have utilized this tool and expressed their appreciation for its ability to help them to make the right decisions.

Best NQDC Practices

As stated above, NQDC plans can be great vehicles for helping the right companies to attract/ retain top talent. The fact that these plans can be designed in so many ways is one of the reasons these plans tend to be more complicated and that relatively few providers have deep expertise here. While there is no single agreed upon definition as to what constitutes best NQDC practices, we'll share some highlights we've garnered from past experience, as well as a review of sources such as the PlanSponsor Magazine Executive Benefits Survey, Newport Executive Benefits Survey, Clark Survey and an excellent article: "Plan Design Features to Increase Participation in NQDC Plans" (PLANSPONSOR Magazine, 2017) (Newport, 2017) (Clark, 2005) (MacDonald, 2018):

- Participants are allowed to defer some portion of earnings (salary, bonus and sometimes long-term incentives)
- The sponsoring organization provides a competitive, yet reasonable match
- Participants are provided a balanced set of around 12-20 investment choices
- The plan is funded utilizing Corporate-Owned Life Insurance (COLI) or mutual funds or both; a thorough analysis will guide associated decision-making here
- The Plan complies with IRC Section 101(j)
- The organization provides a vesting schedule for participant deferrals
- Participants are provided with flexible distribution options to meet their short, mid, and long-term financial requirements
- A Rabbi Trust is considered to provide additional assurances to the Plan participants
- The Plan providers (e.g. Plan Administrator) are well qualified with proven backgrounds to handle the sponsoring organization's needs
- Excellent training and communications are provided to eligible plan participants, including in person, one-on-one meetings
- The provider team includes a Registered Investment Advisor (RIA) with personal access to the dedicated plan consultants and administrator

Alternative Plan Considerations

The case study referenced at the beginning of this chapter pertains to a Public Company client of ours. NQDC plans are very beneficial to many "C" Corporations, as well as many "S" Corporations.

In the case of another client structured as an "S" corporation, their financial advisors showed the owners how to integrate their existing 401(k) Plan with a Profit Sharing Plan. Because of the demographics associated with their organization, the 2 owner/partners could each sock away about $50,000 per year ($100,000 total) under the integrated plan, which worked with their personal budgets and retirement savings goals.

The Company's actuary also talked with the owners about setting up a Defined Benefit Plan (Pension Plan). While initially skeptical, they listened closely. Here's a bit of what the two owners learned: These plans promise to pay eligible employees specified monthly benefits at retirement. Such plans are formula-driven and may be based upon factors such as salary and service. These plans are tax deductible to the employer and tax-deferred for the participating employees. Depending upon many variables, these plans could provide attractive benefits for the Company's employees and significant capital accumulation for the owners.

Let's look at some of the advantages and disadvantages of a defined benefit plan:

Advantages:

- The Plan provides a predictable benefit, and benefit accumulations can exceed $2M.

- The Plan is tax-deductible for the employer and tax deferred for employees until retirement distributions are made. Employers can contribute more into a Defined Benefit Plan than other qualified plans.
- Any business entity of any size can sponsor one of these plans. These plans can be combined with other qualified plans, like 401(k)/Profit Sharing Plans. The employer can establish eligibility and vesting requirements. The Plan can utilize a wide variety of investment choices.

Disadvantages:

- Annual contributions are required; under certain conditions the plan may be "frozen;" otherwise, an excise tax may be applied if the minimum annual funding requirement is not met.
- Participant assets are pooled, so there are no individual directed accounts. The employer bears the investment risk/ reward.

So, in short, as an "S" Corporation, (like so many private companies), our client benefitted from having the 401(k)/Profit Sharing, as well as the Pension Plan. Each year, the partner/owners continue to work closely with their CPA and Actuary to ensure these plans are properly funded. The Plans have helped the Company's existing employees to save a good bit for retirement and have provided significant tax-advantaged capital accumulation for the partners.

So whether you are a "C" Corporation, an "S" or "LLC," know that there are plans available to benefit the owners, as well as the employees. Each organization, however, has its own unique characteristics, including demographics, and should seek proper guidance from its advisors.

We only wish we would have personally taken advantage of these types of plans earlier.

Chapter 13

Remaining in Compliance

A few years ago, a local attorney, seeking an expert witness, contacted us for a case he was building. The case involved a family-owned C Corporation, in which the CEO was the majority owner, and his non-employee sister was the minority shareholder. The sister had filed a lawsuit against her brother, alleging that he was paying himself an unreasonably large salary and annual bonus.

We quickly learned that there was no love lost between the brother and sister.

You see, in a C Corporation annual wages are not double-taxed like dividends. So each year, the CEO would pay himself a huge salary, and then bonus himself all (or most) of the company's net income. In doing so, this left little to nothing in dividends to split with his sister.

All of our due diligence in researching this case pointed to one thing: the CEO was unreasonably overcompensated. As such, he was not only "ripping off" his sister, but also the IRS! Once the details surrounding this case became more vivid to the attorneys on both sides, the case was quickly settled.

Owners of private companies need to exercise care in how they pay themselves. In essence, payouts of salaries, as well as any bonuses or dividends need to be structured in such a way as to not "shortchange" the Government. Please note, however, that what is considered "unreasonable compensation" depends upon whether the company is a C Corporation or an S Corporation. Also, at the time of this printing, the IRS does not have a uniform set of guidelines for determining reasonable compensation.

In a C corporation, wages paid are deductible by the company and taxed to the employee. However, shareholder dividends are not deductible by the company and are taxed to the employee; therefore, they are double taxed. So when the "employee" is also an owner of the company, he/she may be inclined to take as high a salary and bonus as possible to avoid taking any dividends, thus resulting in the most advantageous personal tax situation. Since this results in less tax paid to the government, the IRS does not look favorably upon this and can actively challenge any salaries or bonuses they believe to be UNREASONABLY high.

S-corporations are pass through entities; so all net income ends up being claimed by the owner(s) of the organization and not the organization itself. So when an employee is also an owner of the company, they may be inclined to take as low of a salary as possible to avoid payroll taxes and simply take the money as a shareholder distribution instead. Since this, again, results in less taxes being paid, it puts the owner at risk of an IRS audit.

Although the "flags" of unreasonable executive compensation are completely opposite for S and C corporations, the solution to the issue is the same. Private companies should do their due diligence in establishing their salaries. These should be within a comparable range of relevant compensation survey market data. Likewise, any bonuses should be reasonable and linked to company performance.

We realize that many private company owners have very aggressive growth goals, which may include going public at some point...if this describes your organization, good for you! Bear in mind, however, that this is an expensive process and doing so may result in your company having to comply with stringent Dodd-Frank legislation and intense scrutiny from Proxy Advisors: Glass-Lewis and Institutional Shareholder Services (ISS).

Chapter 14

Special Considerations- The Family-Owned Business

For many of us, having our own business typifies the "American Dream;" and why not: no boss, the ability to create our own product or service; and, perhaps the opportunity to make some really big bucks. Oh yes, I almost forgot about lifetime employment and the possibility of leaving a real legacy. Wow, sounds too good to be true. Well, in many cases it certainly is! According to Bloomberg, 8 out of 10 entrepreneurial businesses fail during their first 18 months. Many of these simply implode.

Let's take a moment to share a story that depicts the thinking and inner workings of many family enterprises. A few years ago, I (Larry) was asked to meet with the executive team of a family-owned global corporation. While the Company had enjoyed excellent growth and become a major global player, they had recently hit a wall. Following the passing of the CEO (father), serious conflicts began to occur between family members which adversely affected the other senior leadership team members.

Family-owned organizations often resist "outsiders." In fact, when I was introduced to the COO, he looked me in the eye and said: "I hate consultants!" Wow, this was going to be a fun engagement!

Even so, we ultimately got the gig and were able to come up with an executive compensation plan that everyone agreed to. The real fun began when we got the team to commit to building a strong "pay for performance" culture. As part of this initiative, we aligned and focused the rest of the company through our customized Goalsharing methodology. I'm happy to say that all but one of the Company goals was significantly overachieved. More importantly, the culture was restored, engagement significantly improved, and the foundation was laid for future success.

It would be nice if all such stories had happy endings, but family businesses can be heaven...or they can be hell.

While no two family organizations are exactly alike, we'd like to share some guidelines for navigating executive compensation through this type of privately held organization:

1. Begin with the end in mind. The family should have a clear vision of the desired future state. For instance, are they most interested in business continuity to retain the family business for future generations...or are they more interested in building wealth and cashing out? Even if they pursue the former route, they should have a process in place for determining what to do in the event they receive an offer that's too hard to refuse.

2. Craft a clear-cut compensation positioning philosophy with an appropriate set of associated program objectives. This establishes the foundation for the executive compensation program. Review these periodically to ensure that all of the key stakeholders remain on the same page.

3. Create the appropriate organizational structure and map out how this is expected to evolve mid and long-term. Ensure that executive roles are staffed with highly qualified, well-suited individuals with complementary skills. Where roles can be filled appropriately with family members, that can be a plus. Keep in mind, however, that these roles are most critical to the organization and, as such, inappropriate selection can be costly and limiting.

4. Establish a strong Board of Directors or Board of Advisors to guide the company's strategic direction. Select an odd number of board members to facilitate decision-making. Incorporate a Compensation Committee to enhance the

quality and objectivity of associated "go forward" pay considerations.

5. Aside from having an overall compensation positioning philosophy, clarify the purpose of each of the respective total compensation components: base pay, short-term incentive pay, long-term incentive pay, and any executive benefits/ perks.

6. Refer to the appropriate chapters of this book to help in determining important criteria for establishing short and long-term incentive plans. Keep in mind that many family companies shy away from offering stock to executives, but are often open to phantom stock or long-term cash- based alternatives.

7. Avoid executive perks that emphasize status differential, opting instead for those that are practical, well perceived and cost effective (e.g. executive physicals, health club memberships, low-cost financial/ legal counseling, executive deferral plans).

8. Take the time to carefully communicate the workings of your executive compensation program. Research indicates that most executives don't fully understand the purpose and workings of their programs--- what a shame! Naturally, executives can't be as motivated/ committed if they don't understand their plans.

9. Interview a few executive compensation firms prior to arriving at your selected advisor. Beware of those who produce fancy charts and graphs, but are ill- equipped to develop effective pay-for-performance solutions.

10. Review your program each year and re-benchmark your roles at least bi-annually. The world of executive compensation is extremely dynamic and the market for top talent remains acute.

Chapter 15

Special Considerations- The Non-Profit Organization

Over the years, one of the most common statements in Corporate Annual Reports has been the phrase: "People are our greatest asset." Recently, this seems to have changed to "our BEST people are our greatest asset." It's important to recognize that the war for talent is not restricted to publicly-traded or privately held corporations. Non-profit organizations are also tasked with bringing in top-notch leaders. However, these types of organizations are unable to provide lavish stock grants or excessive bonuses. They are held to a higher standard in terms of providing reasonable compensation. Failing to do so can prove very costly. Excessive executive compensation can trigger an official IRS inquiry or even an examination (audit). Additionally, should the IRS find overpayment, the non-profit could lose its tax -exempt status, as well as levy hefty fines on the persons involved. So, what does the IRS allow:

According to GuideStar 2015:

"The IRS allows tax-exempt organizations to pay executives "reasonable compensation." There is no universal standard defining reasonable, however. What's reasonable at one non-profit may be a gross under-or overpayment at another. The organizations must determine appropriate salary and benefits packages based on the following considerations:

- They can pay their executives market rate
- Market rate is determined by researching what someone in a similar position would earn at an organization that is of the same size and has a similar mission or field of activity
- They can look at non-profit and for-profit compensation when determining market rate, as long

as the job, organization, size and organization mission/ purpose are comparable

- The IRS has no standard formula, such as percentage of total revenues or expenses for determining compensation, nor are there any tables or schedules that define reasonable compensation
- Per the 2018 Tax Reform, any compensation to an executive in excess of $1M will trigger an excise tax of 21% to the organization

In years gone by, it was less common for non-profit organizations to provide bonuses to their executives. All of this has changed, as this is becoming an increasingly prevalent practice among non-profit organizations. Again, however, non-profits need to be prudent in ensuring that such bonuses are reasonable and appropriate. Below are some guidelines/ considerations we put together for some of our non-profit clients to guide them in this area:

- Bonus plan is established by an independent Board of Directors or by an independent Compensation Committee. The Executive Director can be a member of the Board, but the majority of the Board/ Compensation Committee should be comprised of independent directors.
- Bonus plan is the result of arm's length bargaining
- Bonus plan is reasonable in terms of the employee's specialty, geographic locale, and industry, and based upon services the executive actually performs
- Bonus plan includes a ceiling or reasonable maximum annualized payout target. While Short-term Incentive Plans in the For-Profit Sector often include upside potential beyond a "Target" bonus, this practice is often frowned upon within the Non-Profit Sector. The "Target" level should be reasonable maximum, considering the executive's specialty and his/her total compensation package

- Bonus plan takes into account measures of the employee's performance. The bonus can be tied to one or more performance measures, which can be weighted based upon relative importance. Such performance measures should be linked to criteria that are deemed important to the non-profit organization. Sample performance categories include growth, meeting budget, customer satisfaction and quality/ongoing improvement
- Bonus plan does not have the potential to reduce the charitable services or benefits the organization would otherwise provide
- Bonus plan keeps the organization within budget without having to charge more for services
- Bonus plan does not transform the principal activity of the organization into a joint venture between it and the employee
- Bonus plan is not merely a device to distribute all or a portion of the organization's profits to persons who are in control of the organization; while executives of non-profit organizations should be paid fairly, they are expected to put aside their interests for personal gain for the betterment of the organization
- Bonus plan does not result in abuse or unwarranted benefits

In terms of drafting the bonus plan, we recommend that the plan be written and include a number of pertinent criteria, such as:

- The purpose and description of the plan
- The effective date of the plan (e.g. January- December XXXX)
- Who the plan covers and any pertinent eligibility criteria
- The maximum annualized incentive payout target

- Performance goal(s) and any associated weightings
- Criteria for determining whether or not the performance goal(s) was achieved
- Timing of any bonus payment
- How the payment will be made (e.g. direct deposit)
- How changes of employment status will affect any bonus payouts:
    - New hire during the course of the plan year
    - Voluntary resignation
    - Promotion, transfer, demotion
    - Death, disability, leave of absence
    - Termination "for cause"
    - Termination "not for cause"
    - Elimination of position

Chapter 16

Special Considerations- The Publicly Traded Company

A few years ago, the CHRO of a prominent publicly traded company asked us to review their company's executive compensation program. Apparently, the Board had their own favorite executive compensation advisor, but the HR team had developed some reservations and wanted another set of eyes to ensure that their plan was meeting their expectations. At the time, the "Say on Pay" component of Dodd Frank was getting a lot of attention and publicly traded companies were experiencing a great deal of scrutiny from Proxy Advisors, ISS and Glass Lewis. One of the first things we discovered was that the Company had received "D" ratings during the last 2 years from ISS (largely reflecting a concerning relationship between executive pay and performance) and that receiving one more "D" rating could lead the institutional advisors to giving a "no" vote relative to the "Say on Pay" provision…a score relatively few publicly traded companies receive nowadays. We found a number of other issues, and were later asked to create new short and long-term incentive plans that incented the appropriate performance and behavior, while yielding reasonable compensation levels with strong pay-for-performance relationships.

As an HR leader, you may have an opportunity to play a role in managing executive compensation in a publicly traded company. If so, you'll probably find the role intellectually stimulating as well as challenging in terms of the board members you could end up supporting. You may also experience a level of greed that you've never experienced or imagined. Regardless, you will want to ensure that you are competent and confident in assuming these complex responsibilities.

The executive compensation role can seem overwhelming at times. With that in mind, let us suggest some key tips for carrying out this role.

1. Review the Executive Compensation Charter. This illustrates how executive compensation decisions will be made. If nothing is in place, this is a key starting point and a requirement for all NYSE and NASDAQ companies

2. Ensure all key stakeholders are on the same page in terms of the company's compensation positioning philosophy and associated program objectives

3. Comply with the SEC which requires the company to disclose whether it has any compensation policies and practices (for executives and non-executives) that give rise to risks that are reasonably likely to have a "material affect" on the company. Generally, this is something you, as the CHRO, may work on with the company's CFO and General Counsel

4. Create clear-cut role descriptions that clarify the incumbent executives' roles, backgrounds and qualifications. This is especially helpful to Compensation Committee members of the Board who are not intimately familiar with what these individuals bring to the party. This is also helpful in providing a foundation for associated decision-making pertaining to any recommendations for changes to base, short, and/ or long-term compensation

5. Develop or review the company's existing "peer group" for benchmarking purposes. Such peer groups are generally comprised of 12-20 companies of comparable size (1/2 to 2x revenue) and industry. Utilize the approved peer group for benchmarking the company's pay and financial performance against the peer group

6. Consider supplementing the peer group analysis with a separate market analysis utilizing appropriate benchmarking parameters and a highly respected external survey data source(s)

7. Be proactive and accessible in providing any other appropriate company and compensation- related

information to ensure thorough and effective benchmarking analysis

8. Be sure to also include benchmarks pertaining to executive benefits/ perquisites, in addition to base, short, and long-term compensation

9. Be prepared to provide your own considerations and applicable recommendations

10. Since this process is often a bit "herky-jerky" in companies, take the initiative to propose an action plan laying out what needs to be done each year, to ensure all related requirements are completed in an effective, efficient, and timely manner.

Chapter 17

Special Considerations- The High-Tech Start-up

It has been said that "a team has succeeded in splitting up equity if all of the co-founders are equally unhappy."

.

Last year, we were invited to meet with the Senior Leadership Team of an exciting new start-up company. The founder had hired a well-qualified and inspirational CEO, who, in turn, hired the COO and CMO. While the subject of equity sharing had been broached, the team got caught up in the other priorities/ urgencies of launching the enterprise, and subsequently delayed related discussions---big mistake!

Once such equity discussions resumed, it became immediately clear that the leaders were miles apart. The owner, (who didn't play an active role in the operations) felt that, since his family came up with the service concept, he was entitled to the "lion's share" of the equity. On the other hand, since the CEO, COO and CMO were tasked with building out the infrastructure and driving the company forward, they believed that they should receive most of the equity.

By the time we were called in, the team had already engaged another consulting firm and then an outside mediator, with no agreed-upon solution. After we conducted our own interviews and a comprehensive analysis, we provided our recommendations. The team then agreed to "lock themselves in a room" until they reached a consensus. Happily, after two hours the problem was resolved.

The above case study by no means intends to minimize the complexity involved in getting equity right. Quite the contrary, as there are no universally agreed upon models for establishing equity levels. A number of variables need to be considered, such as: who are the founders? Have they personally invested any of their own monies? What, if any, role will these individuals have moving forward? Is this a family organization, in which business continuity/ legacy may be a priority or is the primary goal to aggressively build the performance, value and attractiveness of the enterprise for a change of control? Are the founders qualified to take the company to subsequently higher levels? Will initial roles and equity levels be expected to shift in the future and how? What other executives may need to be hired and when? Will these executives also be expecting equity and, if so, how much? Should all employees be eligible for some level of equity, or will equity be reserved for key/ long-term strategic contributors and perhaps some "hot skills" employees? What types of outside investment may be needed at what stages, and how will this affect short and early-stage equity levels?

While these types of organizations have their distinct challenges, many of our earlier tips and considerations apply, such as:

1. Begin with the end in mind. What does the company's "end game" look like?

2. Craft a clear-cut compensation positioning philosophy with an appropriate set of associated program objectives. Determine the role each component of compensation plays at various stages of the organization's evolution. Consider the organization's ability to pay and what the competition may be offering for these types of roles. While not universally the case, often times in start-ups base compensation is low to market, but is offset with larger equity/ long-term compensation stakes. However, as the company grows, it is not unusual to see later hires receiving larger salary offers than their counterparts who joined earlier on. This can become very problematic and it is important to develop a game plan for mitigating/ addressing such issues in advance

3. Clarify initial and anticipated roles for benchmarking purposes and associated analysis

4. Consider establishing a strong Board of Directors or Board of Advisors to guide the company's strategic direction. Incorporate a Compensation Committee to enhance the quality and objectivity of associated "go forward" considerations

5. Take the time to carefully communicate the workings of your compensation program

6. Consider engaging an executive advisor who has proven expertise in this "space" and can help at various stages of the company's evolution. Ask your advisor to model out a variety of pertinent equity sharing scenarios to provide the company's decision makers with a number of alternatives, along with the pros/ cons of each

7. Review your program frequently as the high-tech world is extremely dynamic

Chapter 18

What to Do Now?

"Intelligence is taking something complicated and making it simple."
C.W. Ceram

The above quote is not only one of our favorites, but has been a guiding principle in how we have operated our business over the last few decades.

There is no shortage of Executive Compensation books on the market. However, many are 300-1000+ pages, too detailed, and overly theoretical. We realize that in your role as the organization's HR Leader, you will need to be confident and competent in carrying out any related Executive Compensation responsibilities and may need to get up to speed quickly!

We also realize that it isn't likely that you will actually sit down and study one of these voluminous compensation books. For this reason, we wrote this concise, executive compensation guide and incorporated proven case studies, practical tips, humorous stories and anecdotes to improve your level of engagement and understanding.

You can read the book in its entirety in about 90 minutes…or you can zoom in on any chapters you find most relevant.

Of course, we all realize that a little knowledge can be a dangerous thing. This is especially true in the world of executive compensation, which continues to evolve rapidly. For this reason, should you have any questions at any time, drop us an email, or give us a call.

Larry Comp and Steve Smith

LTC Performance Strategies, Inc.
28001 Smyth Drive, Suite 103
Valencia, CA 91355
(661) 294-2929

lcomp@ltcperformance.com
ssmith@ltcperformance.com

www.ltcperformance.com

LTC Performance Strategies, Inc., is independently owned and operated. Securities offered through the Leaders Group, Inc., member FINRA/SIPC, 26 West Dry Creek Circle, Suite #575, Littleton, CO 80120, (303) 797-9080

Sample Philosophy and Objectives Statement

Executive Compensation Program

Compensation Positioning Philosophy

- We offer attractive total compensation opportunities for significant company & individual performance

Program Objectives

- Attract & retain top caliber, well-suited executives

- Incent the desired company/ team/ individual performance & behavior, while ensuring a strong pay-for-performance relationship

- Consider key variables (e.g. organization's size, stage of evolution, geographical markets) in designing optimal Total Compensation Program

- Be externally competitive, internally equitable and consistent in administration

- Ensure organizational roles are clear, yet appropriately flexible

- Ensure titles reflect roles and are positively perceived

- Provide appropriate opportunities for personal/ professional development and meaningful contribution

- Contain rising employee benefit costs while providing highly perceived offerings

- Provide executive perquisites that offer income protection, tax savings and investment vehicles, as appropriate

- Comply with applicable local, state & federal legislation

- Ensure the program is flexible to adapt to changing business & organizational circumstances

- Ensure the program is simple to administer & easy to understand

- Ensure the program is cost effective and provides a solid return on investment (ROI)

Appendix B

Sample Job Description

Job Description

Company: XYZ Company
Position: President & COO
Location: Los Angeles, CA
Department: Executive
Reporting to: CEO
FLSA Status: Exempt

General Purpose
Responsible for the profitable revenue growth, and the effective, efficient and ethical operation of the company, in line with its mission, vision and values.

Responsibilities
Essential functions of the job are listed below. Other responsibilities may also be assigned. Please note that the essential functions may vary depending on department size, organizational structure and/or geographic location. Reasonable accommodations may be made to allow differently-abled individuals to perform the essential functions of the job.

- Provides strategic direction and oversight in guiding the organization in achieving its goals for profitable revenue growth, increased shareholder value/ liquidity, and long-term organizational health.
- Guides development of strategic planning process and annual business plan in line with the organization's long-term vision.
- Monitors economic and industry trends; identifies growth opportunities, as well as potential threats to the organization. Assesses the strengths and weaknesses of other companies (competitors and non-competitors) in architecting a path to dominate strategic sectors.
- Plans, develops, and implements strategies used to generate new sources of revenue and opportunities for increased profitability. Seeks out and develops mutually beneficial partnerships.
- Partners with CEO in identification and diligence of acquisition and merger opportunities. Plans and directs associated implementation activities.
- Reviews activity reports and financial statements in tracking progress toward short and longer-term goals and objectives; takes corrective actions as needed.
- Ensures that the appropriate systems, programs, policies, and procedures are in place and that the organization complies with relevant legal mandates.

- Oversees Company operations to insure efficiency, quality service, and cost-effective management of resources. Provides oversight of vendor selection processes and desired outcomes, and negotiates key contracts for the Company.
- Ensures that the organization has the appropriate structure and right number of properly trained staff to carry out the organization's mission.
- Evaluates management's performance for compliance with established policies and objectives, and contributions towards goal attainment.
- Develops effective leadership team and plans for succession at various levels. Serves as a role model to direct reports and coaches/counsels effectively to build effective leadership throughout the organization.
- Ensures effective corporate communication across the organization, including a unified presentation of leadership, and transmission of key strategic initiatives and other pertinent messages.
- Builds fundraising network utilizing personal contacts and involvement in special events and foundation support.
- Represents Company at legislative sessions, committee meetings, and formal functions.
- Promotes Company through personal appearances at conferences and to local, regional, national and international constituencies.
- Presents Company performance reports at Annual Stockholder and Board of Directors meetings.
- Handles various other duties as delegated by CEO and BOD.
- Carries out all responsibilities in an honest, ethical and professional manner.

Supervisory Responsibilities
In accordance with applicable policies/procedures and Federal/State laws, may perform the following supervisory responsibilities: Interviewing, hiring, orienting, and training employees; planning, assigning, and directing work; coaching and appraising performance; rewarding and disciplining employees; addressing complaints and resolving problems.

Minimum Qualifications
The following are the minimum qualifications that an individual needs in order to successfully perform the duties and responsibilities of this position. Please note that the minimum qualifications may vary based upon the department size and/or geographic location.

Knowledge
- Equivalent of a Bachelor's Degree and 15+ years progressively responsible, related background, including proven experience in comparable senior leadership roles
- Keen understanding of the industry, including the ability to assess the strengths and weaknesses of competitor organizations, recognize and seek out relevant opportunities,

and implement processes for improved efficiency, service, profitability, and growth.
- PC skills

Skills/ Abilities
- Ability to think strategically, synthesize the most complex business/financial data and develop innovative solutions
- Excellent planning, organizing, negotiating and leadership/supervisory skills; ability to focus/ align organization around critical initiatives and facilitate progressive change
- Strong staffing, development and appraisal skills
- Entrepreneurial spirit and willingness to take prudent risks
- Excellent verbal, written and executive presentation skills
- Strong customer, quality and results orientation
- Ability to interact effectively at all levels and break down barriers across departments/ diverse cultures
- Ability to be an effective member of and lead the most complex project teams

Physical Demands
In general, the following physical demands are representative of those that must be met by an employee to successfully perform the essential functions of this job. Reasonable accommodations may be made to allow differently-abled individuals to perform the essential functions of the job.

Must be able to see, hear, speak and write clearly in order to communicate with employees and/or other customers; manual dexterity required for occasional reaching and lifting of small objects, and operating office equipment. Travels as required to meet accountabilities.

Work Environment
In general, the following conditions of the work environment are representative of those that an employee encounters while performing the essential functions of this job. Reasonable accommodations may be made to allow differently-abled individuals to perform the essential functions of the job within the environment.

The office is clean, orderly, properly lighted and ventilated. Noise levels are considered low to moderate.

Sample Mini-Job Profiles

Job Title	Major Responsibilities	Minimum Qualifications
Chief Executive Officer	Responsible for providing strategic vision, shaping the organizational culture, guiding the profitable revenue growth, and facilitating the effective, efficient and ethical operation of the company, in line with its mission and organizational values. Plans, develops and implements long-term growth strategies used to generate new sources of revenue and opportunities for increased profitability. while sustaining positive cash flow. Ensures that the appropriate systems, programs, policies and procedures are in place and that the organization complies with relevant legal mandates	Equivalent of a Bachelor's degree and 15+ years progressively responsible, related background, including proven experience in comparable senior leadership roles. Ability to think strategically, synthesize the most complex business/ financial data and develop innovative solutions. Excellent planning, organizing, negotiating and leadership skills. Ability to focus and align the organization around critical initiatives and facilitate progressive change. Strong staffing, mentoring, development and appraisal capabilities, along with proven verbal, written and executive presentation skills. Strong entrepreneurial spirit and willingness to take prudent risks.

Job Title	Major Responsibilities	Minimum Qualifications
Director, Marketing and Communications	Responsible for the organization's marketing and communications strategy and implementation, including: Brand/ message integrity, website design and content, print and online advertising, video development and production, social networking, special events, online store products, quarterly newsletter, monthly e-blast and organizational-wide campaigns. Recommends, directs, and implements improved systems, policies, and materials for communication and marketing efforts. Selects, orients, trains and manages staff members as appropriate.	Equivalent of a Bachelor's degree and 7-10+ years progressively responsible, related experience. Proven, related Marketing and Communications track record in a progressive environment that has experienced dynamic change and evolution. Excellent planning, organizing, negotiating and leadership skills. Strong staffing, mentoring, development and appraisal capabilities, along with proven verbal, written and executive presentation skills.

Works Cited

(SHRM), S. M. (2018, August 16). 2019 Salary Budgets Inch
    Upward Ever So Slightly.
Bain Consulting. (n.d.). Survey of Senior Executives Pertaining to
    Initiatives that Deliver The Best Financial Results.
Beek, M. (n.d.). The Real Cost of Hiring Average Performers.
Clark. (2005). NQDC Survey.
Economic Research Institute. (2013, 3 1). Executive, Salary &
    Geographic Assessors .
Economic Research Institute. (2018, August). Executive
    Compensation Assessor.
Forum, H. L. (2018).
Harvard. (2018). Law School Forum .
Hollon, J. (2013, 5 23). Survey: Half of Companies Report Higher
    Turnover Than Last Year. *TLNT*.
MacDonald, W. L. (2018). Plan Design Features to Increase
    Participation in NQDC Plans.
Miller, S. (2012, 8 15). Unanimity on 2013 Salary Forecasts Holding
    Up. *Society for Human Resource Management*.
Natitional Institute of Standards & Technology. (2001, 8 27).
    Malcolm Baldrige National Quality Award 1995 Recipient
    Corning Telecommunications Products Division.
Newport. (2017). Executive Benefits Survey.
Petrecca, L., & Strauss, G. (2012, 5 15). CEOs stumble over ethics
    violations, mismanagement. *USA Today*.
PLANSPONSOR Magazine. (2017). Executive Benefits Survey.
Sturman, M. (2003). *Evaluating the Utility of Performance-Based
    Pay*.
Wikipedia. (n.d.). Springfield Remanufacturing.
WorldatWork. (2016). *Private Company Incentive Pay Practices.*

Made in the USA
San Bernardino, CA
09 January 2019